A New Connection

A New Connection

Reforming The United Methodist Church

ANDY LANGFORD &
WILLIAM H. WILLIMON

ABINGDON PRESS
Nashville

A NEW CONNECTION
REFORMING THE UNITED METHODIST CHURCH

Copyright © 1995 by Abingdon Press

All rights reserved.

This book is printed on recycled, acid-free paper.

Library of Congress Cataloging-in-Publication Data

Langford, Andy.
   A new connection : reforming the United Methodist Church / Andy Langford & William H. Willimon.
     p. cm.
   Includes bibliographical references.
   ISBN 0-687-01542-1 (alk. paper)
     1. United Methodist Church (U.S.)—Government. 2. Methodist Church—United States—Government. 3. Church renewal—Methodist Church. I. Willimon, William H. II. Title.
   BX8388.L36 1996
   262'.076—dc20
                                        95-46391
                                            CIP

Scripture quotations are from the New Revised Standard Version Bible, copyright © 1989, by the Division of Christian Education of the National Council of the Churches of Christ in the United States of America.

95 96 97 98 99 00 01 02 03 04 — 10 9 8 7 6 5 4 3 2 1

MANUFACTURED IN THE UNITED STATES OF AMERICA

To
JOHN WESLEY

a reformer of the Church of England

Contents

Acknowledgments

BETWEEN THE TWO OF US, we have visited almost every annual conference of our denomination. In our workshops and seminars throughout the connection, we have met with thousands of United Methodist pastors and laypersons. We thank all those pastors and laity who worked on, thought through, and debated many of the ideas in this book. Special thanks go to members of the Lilly Endowment/Duke Divinity School Study of United Methodism and American Culture within which an original paper on this topic was written by Andy. We also thank our colleagues in the Western North Carolina and South Carolina annual conferences who have encouraged us in this journey. Special appreciation goes to the Western North Carolina Annual Conference, which approved 154 petitions to the 1996 General Conference. These experiences, along with our deep concern and love for our church, motivated us to write this book.

Introduction

COME, LET US REASON TOGETHER

THE TIME HAS COME for United Methodists to talk of many things, of mission and church, of boards and money, of consultation and appointments, of districts and jurisdictions, of bishops and the laity. The time has come to speak with candor and courage and hope.

The time has come. United Methodism is no longer effectively organized to achieve its missional goals. We are living with an outdated denominational structure that came into being at another time to achieve different intentions.

Our present organization was a creature of that time (1968–72) when inherited and established authorities in North American life were being challenged and when new forms were being tentatively developed. The openness was good, the effort to think anew about how to structure the church was commendable. Both the Evangelical United Brethren and the Methodists had much to contribute.

Given the times and the dominant ideas, the trend was to create a large bureaucracy, to think in terms of the general church and of leadership being provided from the top of an organizational hierarchy to have power among many persons. But the times have changed.

The organization produced in the early seventies no longer serves us well. In national political life, in business organizations, in charitable institutions, and in churches we have learned that all of the assumptions of even that recent past were time-limited and worked against contemporary sensibilities and missional mandates. We need a new order. It is not true that the arrangements are good, that all we need are good people to fill the established roles. Even good people cannot overcome malformed systems. The structure of the church needs to be changed.

Clarity of vision and purposeful order of priorities are our prime necessities. The church must serve our people, not our people the church; local decision making and contribution must be enhanced; bureaucracy must be reduced; episcopal leadership must be reestablished; our organizational form must be fitted to our missional function.

Most of all we must be open to the leading of the Holy Spirit. We must be open to surprising new discoveries and to renewable organizational formation. There is no structural panacea, no one form that will now and forever serve The United Methodist Church. We want to explore ways to achieve present possibilities and to answer present problems. We hope to allow constructive thought and creative change in United Methodism to provide more latitude for action and the possibility of more rapid and appropriate responses to our changing society. The time has come to talk, to open conversation in honest love within our church about organizational liabilities in our present structure, and to think about changes that will enhance our mission and our life together as "a people called Methodists."

The recognition of problems is a sensitive matter. Exposed nerves will be touched. Yet naming our difficulties can be therapeutic. Criticism offered in a spirit of constructive, heartfelt concern can be helpful. It is our intention to be sharply critical, but fair, and to challenge the status quo. It is also our intention to be positive about prospects and to express the hope that reformation will lead to renewal.

In speaking about the future of our beloved United Methodist Church today it is difficult to overstate the present situation. Nearly a decade ago, *Rekindling the Flame* reached for the language of crisis in attempting to grab the attention of United Methodists:

> The United Methodist Church faces a crisis unequaled to any since the schism preceding the Civil War. The continued membership decline is the major symptom of this crisis, but the issues are deeper and more complex than the loss of members. In any organization, when things are not going well, there are always those who urge silence, unquestioning loyalty, and the suppression of all criticism. But our church is too important to be allowed to wither.[1]

For the most part, the alarmist language of that book and its specific proposals for renewal—along with numerous other books and papers by pastors, bishops, and laity— have gone unheeded by the leaders of our church. There were no fundamental changes in the way our church works; our connection lost another half million members. The time was not right for change. The crisis worsened. Our concern is not new. In 1968, the great Wesleyan theologian Albert Outler warned the newly formed denomination that the proposed structure would dissipate power, create an isolated bureaucracy, and alienate local congregations.[2] Unfortunately, Outler was correct.

Transformation or change is painful. An old world must be relinquished if a new one is to be born. So the Christian faith has always spoken of conversion, change, and *metanoia* as a gift of a loving, living God rather than merely human achievement. Left to our own devices, an individual or a whole church will plod along the accustomed path rather than venture forth. Yet Easter proclaims that our God is a God of the living rather than the dead (Luke 20:38). Always out ahead of us, our God calls to us from the edge of the future, "I am about to do a new thing; now it springs forth, do you not perceive it?" (Isaiah 43:19).

John Wesley's "people called Methodists" were born out of the surprising new thing that God worked in eighteenth-century England. God used Evangelical United Brethren and Methodists to teach the world to "sing to the LORD a new song" (Isaiah 42:10). We believe God can use us again.

Therefore our models and our heroes must not be those who seek safe harbors, who fail to risk, who refuse to think new things, or who are unable to trust God. The first step on the way forward may be a look back at the way of old Abraham and Sarah, reluctant Moses, and surprised Mary. Our hope is not in ourselves and our resources, although we believe the human and material resources within United Methodism are great. Our hope is in a living Lord who made heaven and earth, and in Jesus Christ, who, having called each of us to be his disciple, is able to work within us more than we dare to dream.

A number of our friends reviewed the manuscript for this book and said that it is "a huge political gamble," whatever that means. Yet we must speak. Why? Because we want to move beyond talk to action, beyond theoretical discourse to disciplinary language. We speak because we believe that United Methodism is destined for more than unmitigated decline. The imperatives of the gospel still apply to us. Human need for the gospel is as great as ever. We love our church and believe that God still has plans to use United Methodism, if United Methodism is willing to let God use us. In God's great scheme of things, we believe the time is right for our church to make bold, creative, missionally motivated moves, similar to the bold moves that gave birth to our denomination over two hundred years ago.

Come, let us reason together, let us think about our United Methodist Church, let us look our denomination straight in the eye, but also let us recognize that God is always about doing new things and that some of these new things can be done through United Methodism.

And best of all, God is with us.

Andy Langford
William H. Willimon
Pentecost, 1995

Disciplinary paragraphs related to the problems we identify in this book appear in shaded areas, with suggested additions in boldface and suggested deletions crossed through.

Chapter 1

REVITALIZE THE CONNECTION

WE RECALL THE BISHOP who said, "The more I think about the larger church—General Conference, even annual conference—the more depressed I become. The more I focus upon the witness of the local congregation, the better I feel." We agree.

Today, thousands of United Methodist congregations are thriving. Each week, they reach out to persons in the name of Jesus Christ, they nurture people in Christian discipleship, they open up the riches of God's Word in relevant ways, and they send out disciples to transform the world. These congregations demonstrate God's loving action toward the world.

Typical of these thriving congregations are the churches named by the Western North Carolina Conference as "Churches of Excellence." Over one hundred churches, just under 10 percent of the total congregations in the conference, have been named "Churches of Excellence" over the past few years. These are congregations that are "servant-like, simple, sincere, inclusive, uncompromising, stewardly, and assert excellence." Each of these vital congregations

— started a new Sunday school class
— increased Sunday school attendance
— conducted a confirmation class
— received persons into membership by profession of faith
— paid all apportioned funds in full
— conducted an annual stewardship campaign
— increased weekly attendance by 5 percent
— had an active youth ministry
— had a new self-initiated program for the church
— created a new missional ministry
— participated in a mission program beyond the local church

These churches include congregations that are small and large, rural and urban, in declining communities and in growing suburbs, and with people of every color. Some have women as pastors; some have men as pastors; some are served by clergy couples. These congregations initiated programs in children's ministry, clown ministry, Habitat for Humanity, after-school care, prayer groups, lay visitation, seeker worship services, evangelistic mission teams, and the list continues.

Curiously, the conference is not quite sure what to do with such churches. The first year, the "Churches of Excellence" were recognized at a special session during annual conference. But simultaneously a number of clergy and laity (in congregations that did not qualify) complained that the criteria were too high, that the conference was just "playing a numbers game." As leaders of each church of excellence came forward to be congratulated by the bishop, one could feel the discomfort in the conference among the majority, those who simply maintained the status quo. Last year, possibly because of such unrest, the annual conference simply handed out small plaques to the "Churches of Excellence" during registration.

In these congregations, and many more throughout the world, The United Methodist Church is alive and well. Why should we be threatened by them? There is an unfortunate dynamic, which sometimes plagues troubled organizations. Amid decline, stories of growth, newness, and success can be threatening. The old order needs to believe that decline is utterly unmitigated, that God cannot or will not do any new thing among us. By believing this, we can continue in the same old ruts. Yet Easter promises us that God is alive, that the Holy Spirit will not leave us to our own devices, and that the risen Christ may yet have ministry in mind for us. We must believe in Easter.

> The central, focal expression of ministry and mission in the name of Christ is found in the local church congregation.... Here, in the congregation, the gospel must be made real if we expect it to be made real anywhere.
> *The Council of Bishops of The United Methodist Church,* Vital Congregations—Faithful Disciples *(Nashville: Graded Press, 1990), 10*

Decades of Denial

In 1968 the union of the Evangelical United Brethren and the Methodist churches formed the Protestant denomination with the largest number of churches in North America, The United Methodist Church. The merger was very much a product of the times. Bigness was considered to be an asset. The size of the federal government was exploding. It was argued that a larger denomination with more bureaucracy would be more efficient, more effective. We duplicated every structure at the general church down to the local congregation. We dissi-

Graph 1

**United Methodist
Membership
(in millions)**

1969-1993

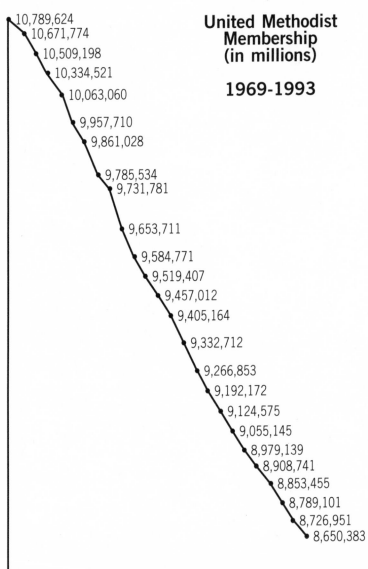

10,789,624
10,671,774
10,509,198
10,334,521
10,063,060
9,957,710
9,861,028
9,785,534
9,731,781
9,653,711
9,584,771
9,519,407
9,457,012
9,405,164
9,332,712
9,266,853
9,192,172
9,124,575
9,055,145
8,979,139
8,908,741
8,853,455
8,789,101
8,726,951
8,650,383

1969 70 71 72 73 74 75 76 77 78 79 80 81 82 83 84 85 86 87 88 89 90 91 92 93

Source of these data: *General Minutes of the Annual Conferences of The United Methodist Church* (Evanston, Ill.: General Council on Finance and Administration, 1969-1993).

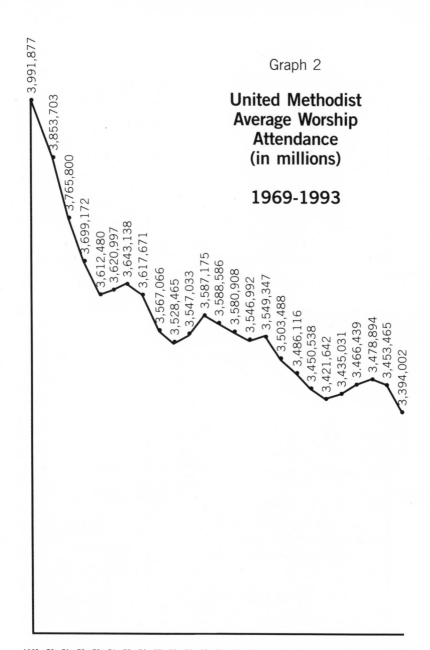

Graph 2

**United Methodist
Average Worship
Attendance
(in millions)**

1969-1993

1969 70 71 72 73 74 75 76 77 78 79 80 81 82 83 84 85 86 87 88 89 90 91 92 93
Source of these data: *General Minutes of the Annual Conferences of The United Methodist Church* (Evanston, Ill.: General Council on Finance and Administration, 1969-1993).

pated power among thirteen general agencies, councils, and commissions. We established apportionments to fund every good idea.

Alas, only a short time after merger, we painfully learned how inefficient and how outmoded the large, bureaucratically administered denomination could be.

The year 1969 is now remembered, not as the exciting first year for the new United Methodist Church, but rather as the beginning of precipitous decline. In less than two decades, we lost about two million members (see graph 1). Over a half million fewer people were attending Sunday worship (see graph 2). We closed an average of nearly four United Methodist churches *every week*.

After solidifying our merger with a new organization in 1972, there have been virtually no fundamental changes in the way our denomination at large is organized and operated.[1] A comparison of our *Discipline* between 1972 and 1994 reveals our frightening inability to modify our mode of operation. The *Discipline* of this period is mainly distinguished by the rapid growth of coercive legislation—rules mandating more committees, more funds derived from our congregations, and more bureaucracy for the general church. At the same time, there have been more regulations and committees in local churches required by the general church. We went from several paragraphs in 1964 on local church stewards, the central administrative body of the congregation, to over *thirty pages* in our 1992 *Discipline* regulating the membership, structure, and duties of the administrative boards or councils, a trend that theologian Albert Outler once dismissed as "benevolent despotism."

The striking unwillingness of our church to address these problems, combined with contemporary Americans' negativity about large, national bureaucracy in any form, has brought us to a crisis of nearly inconceivable proportions. Theological and political controversies divide us. Business within the General Conference and annual conferences is increasingly preoccupied with financial crises. Never before have so many laity and pastors questioned the value of our connection. Our glorious connection is now seen by many, particularly many of the laity, as a huge liability.

Connectionalism has come to be identified with organizational identity and uniformity from top to bottom, and unquestioning service to the present organizational structure. A district superintendent with whom we are acquainted accused a small congregation of being "unchristian" when it balked at supporting the Southeastern Jurisdictional Fund. She was operating under the assumption that only sinful people could question the financial requests of the larger church. When a layperson asked her pastor about the necessity of paying her congregation's apportionments in full, she was told, "Apportionments *are* The United Methodist Church. Anyone who doesn't want to support apportioned askings in full does not want to be a United Methodist."

The tragedy of these statements is that they turn United Methodism on its head, misunderstanding both the mission of the church and the meaning of "connectionalism." As defined by our *Discipline* (¶ 112.3), our "connectional principle" is that we are to be gathered around a common mission, to work in concert to achieve common goals, to support one another, to acknowledge our different contributions to a shared vision, and to rejoice in the unity which we, though many, find in worshiping and serving together. We are "connected" more by common purpose than by organizational rules. Our United Methodist polity *reflects* our connectional life, it does not *create* it. Our polity is our way of being faithful in pursuing our *mission*. The true theological meaning of connectionalism clearly defines "the connectional principle" on the basis of a network of inter-dependent relationships among our congregations.

Criticism of the critics has all too often been our official denominational response to those who criticize business as usual. If you kill the messenger of bad tidings, the message will disappear. The "good" United Methodist pays what the church asks and keeps quiet. New proposals are quickly killed by charges of "creeping congregationalism," or pleas for more sincere efforts to make the present structure work.

Many of our bishops, district superintendents, and bureaucrats, while thinking of themselves as liberal and progressive, have proved to be extremely defensive and conservative in protecting the old order. Of course, the present system put them in authority, so any criticism of the present system is perceived as a personal attack upon them. They are not bad people, but a system based upon distrust, coercion, and authoritarianism has a way of pro-ducing the sort of leaders it demands. We must find a way forward out of our denial. We are declaring that the emperor has no clothes.

A System That Fosters Distrust

Some of the distrust of the connection may be an expres-sion of human sin. Critics charge that contemporary Amer-ican culture is self-centered, narcissistic, and cynical. We care for our own families first and only occasionally reach out further. Persons in authority are distrusted. Some say that the problem is not the system but the people. In other words, if we simply elected better bishops, chose better dis-trict superintendents, recruited better preachers, all would be well. We declare, contrariwise, that it is not our leaders who are at fault, it truly is our current system that has betrayed us.

There's a theory about what happens when an institution hits the wall. The first stage is shock. The second is defensive retreat. The third is acknowledgment. Fourth is adaptation. In my experience the mainline churches . . . have hit a wall. A lot of things they thought would work aren't working. And as far as I can tell, some of the leaders have moved as far as defensive retreat. But an awful lot of people are in total denial. . . . I don't see many signs of acknowledging the depth of the . . . crisis we're in.

Church consultant and theorist Loren Mead, in "Learning points: An interview with Loren Mead," The Christian Century, 23-30 March 1994, 311

We know and care for many of the leaders of our church. As a pastor and a campus minister and divinity school professor, we are part of the system. Our leaders are almost universally able people, well trained and desirous of giving their best to our church and the cause of Christ. This book is not an attack upon our leaders, but rather a critique of our current system and the ways this system hinders our ministry. For every denominational leader who feels unduly criticized in this book, we know that there will be a dozen others who, having felt constrained and burdened by our present structure, will welcome our critique as a show of support. A number of them have helped us shape our proposals. As a bishop in the West told Will, "If you think the local churches are frustrated, you ought to talk to those of us at the top. I never knew deep, disillusioning frustration until I tried to effect some change, some movement in our church as a bishop."

Too often the current system believes that mission is something conceived and directed by someone at the top. The General Conference or a general board or agency decides what the real work of the church is and then informs the lowly local congregation of its responsibility to support financially that work. Who, except those who are incredibly unchristian, could question good work as defined by those at the top? In spite of such misunderstanding, there are notable examples of a spirit of cooperation between the boards and the local congregations. We applaud, for instance, the General Board of Global Ministries' new Russia initiatives, in which local United Methodist congregations are given more direct contact with mission projects in Russia.

While many local congregations have celebrated mission work teams, sending short-term lay volunteers on mission projects throughout the world, our General Board of Global Ministries (GBGM) has been reluctant to endorse this concept. A frustrated bishop who has served on the GBGM told us that the GBGM's reluctance to endorse mission teams enthusiastically is a sign that it believes local churches and leaders are incapable of being in mission. As one GBGM staff person said to Andy, "Don't they understand I could spend all that money more effectively?" The staff member failed to understand the transformative power of mission work teams for the individuals who go and for the congregations who support them.

Distrust of the local congregation has been the largest factor that has led to our massive decline. Imagine an American corporation, or even school or hospital, in which the leaders announced, "We have lost about 20 percent of our clients over the past two decades but we still feel good about what we are doing and see no need for any fundamental change. Those who think otherwise are negative and disloyal."

Any business with that attitude will be out of business shortly. Much of our present denominational thinking is old thinking, a product of the mentality of the 1950s rather than the 1990s. Back in the 1950s, our denomination almost had a monopoly on Protestant religious life—where people could worship and how and when they could worship. Methodist churches were more ubiquitous, even, than United States Post Offices.

To continue the analogy, consider what has happened to the Postal Service in the past two decades. Having lost its monopoly, it struggles to keep up with new competition, technological change, and customer service. United Methodists observe new, young, independent churches springing up everywhere. New forms of clergy training and support are being discovered elsewhere. The old denominational loyalty ("Once a United Methodist, always a United Methodist"), which preserved the church's leadership from having to think creatively about our system or worry about lay reaction, is now virtually nonexistent, particularly among our younger members.

Today's Americans are consumers. While we worry about the effect of consumerism upon our worship and theology and wonder about its ultimate results, a primary result of the consumer mentality is that modern Americans will not tolerate mediocrity. Having seen quality music and preaching on television, they demand more on Sunday morning in their local church. Whenever there appears to be little connection between clergy effectiveness and clergy appointment and advancement, the people lose faith in our leaders. Whenever the Wesleyan system of governance of clergy solely by clergy appears to degenerate into a form of unionism's closed shop with little accountability for poor job performance or even the ability to discipline grossly errant clergy members of the annual conference, the laity desert us in droves.

Alas, The United Methodist Church's structure, our leaders' unresponsiveness to the present crisis, our bureaucracy's cavalier attitude toward its constituency too closely resembles the United States Postal Service. We want a church with some of the vitality and efficiency of UPS.

A Need for New Thinking

It is easier for our leaders to keep the old alive rather than give birth to the new. Most of the energy of our church is expended in administering yesterday's decisions. Our church finds that it is virtually impossible to close unneeded, redundant institutions. Children's homes and church colleges—yesterday's bold ideas—become today's drain on conference funds. It is virtually impossible to get something into the budget and just as difficult to get something out of the budget once it has found a place for itself and hired its cadre of bureaucratic advocates.

At the 1992 General Conference, there was great excitement about the new National Plan for Hispanic Ministries, a ministry focused on creating house churches led by laity in order to minister to and with the exploding Hispanic population in the United States. Yet, when the time came to fund the program, nothing in the current World Service budget could be cut. Therefore, General Conference simply added another apportioned fund: the Mission Initiatives Fund.

Our leaders operate within a system that dooms them to failure. Mediocrity tends to perpetuate itself. For instance, during the time of episcopal elections in the mid-1980s, there was much talk of the need to reverse the membership decline within our church. A friend of ours did a national study of those who were candidates for bishop and found that only a few of these candidates had served a growing congregation in the last decade. Some of the candidates who were elected bishop had *never* served a growing church. We elected women and men to manage our decline rather than lead us toward growth. And they fulfilled our expectations well.

The 1968–1972 "restructuring" of our church was mainly a retrenchment of some of the worst tendencies inherent in our general bureaucracy. Although few, except Albert Outler, gave voice to it, restructuring fundamentally changed our church. In 1968, our movement became an institution where form determined function. There was the perception that our church was reorganized with neutralized bishops, a top-heavy bureaucracy at greater distance from the local constituencies than had been the case in any of our uniting churches, a funding system with little accountability, and a perceived lack of attention to the needs of the local churches. We became saddled by a staff-controlled bureaucracy in thirteen separate general agencies, commissions, and councils distant from local United Methodist congregations. They are run by a management structure more like the failing General Motors of the 1950s than the Saturn Corporation of the 1990s.

The Demise of Denominational Leadership

Most of the tasks performed by a general denomination are tasks that can be and are being done elsewhere. Indeed, as Lyle Schaller and others have pointed out, the replacement structures for denominations are already in place, many of them now functioning in lieu of denominational agencies. Dozens of publishing houses now publish church school curriculum materials. When one of our congregations mobilizes for evangelism, that congregation is likely to turn to *Net Results* for assistance. When a local church becomes concerned about its growth, it just as likely will turn to the independent Alban Institute or the Yokefellow Institute for advice as to our own Section on Evangelism. Maranatha Music produces transparencies of hymns that numerous United Methodist congregations use to supplement our *United Methodist Hymnal.* Most of those who attend the Youth Specialties national youth workers convocations are United Methodists. A number of our congregations, frustrated by the lack of youth ministry emphasis in our denomination, have turned their youth work over to representatives of Young Life. It has been estimated that there are more United

Methodist youth who are active in Young Life than who are active in the youth programs of United Methodist churches.

There was a time when clergy desiring continuing education could turn only to the seminaries for help. Today, only half of our clergy-in-training attend one of our thirteen seminaries, and these seminaries no longer have a monopoly on clergy continuing education. A large number of United Methodists joined Robert Schuller to create Churches Uniting in Global Mission for local and global mission efforts. A United Methodist is its chief administrator. It seems that the only thing for which United Methodist local congregations are dependent upon the denomination is the credentialing of clergy. If our laity lose faith in the ability of the denomination to perform this task well, then major rationale for the denomination is lost.

> When we began our building program, the Field Service unit of the General Board of Global Ministries refused to come for an interview. They sent the least background information on why we should use them, and offered us their services for a non-negotiable fee. Six other companies came for interviews, provided extensive information about their work, and were willing to negotiate prices. Did our congregation hesitate to choose an independent firm? Of course not. Why do we have such a program of the General Board of Global Ministries, especially one so out of touch with the congregations that fund it?
>
> *A pastor in Pennsylvania*

We are convinced that God will not give us a new church with a renewed sense of mission as long as we remain in denial. Denial is never a source of creative thinking and action. The first step for us is that courageous move out of denial, forward into the faith that God really can work wonders among us, even us. We need new thinking.

Decentralization Is the Key

Nationally and internationally, in politics and business, health care and education, our culture is going through a vast process of decentralization. Organizations that previously functioned with power and decisions flowing from the top down are being broken apart. More decisions are taking place at the grassroots. Public education explores "site-based management," in which teachers and parents are given a greater say in the management of local schools. The United States government, especially after the 1994 election, is becoming decentralized. Alice Rivlin of the Clinton Administration endorses this move and calls it "the new federalism." Business embraces "Total Quality Management," sensing that efficiency and productivity grow when workers feel they have a stake in the success and a say in the direction of the corporation and its products.

The contrast between the old way of thinking and the new way is similar to a comparison of a hologram to a patchwork quilt. Our current system is like a hologram. A hologram is a three-dimensional picture that consists of intersecting rays of light. If a hologram is cut in half, each half still contains the full picture. Cut into thirty-seven thousand pieces, each is the same as the original. Today, our system assumes that every area of interest at the general level must be duplicated in thirty-seven thousand United Methodist congregations worldwide. Our dream is, instead, for a system that is a patchwork quilt consisting of pieces of fabric of different shapes, sizes, colors, and patterns sewn together into a whole. Each individual piece has its own integrity, yet sewn together the pieces form a beautiful whole. Each congregation must have its own mission, administrative structure, financial structure, and leadership, yet, when bound together with thin threads, a wonderful, colorful mosaic is created.

At our best, our church knows that power flows "from the bottom up," from the local church upward throughout the rest of the church. Our bishops affirm local congregations. All our agencies pay lip service to the centrality of the local church. The greatest strength of the new National Plan for Hispanic Ministries is its focus on starting house churches with lay leadership. While a number of church leaders wanted to insist on defining how these house churches would be organized and related to our general church, and others wanted only seminary-trained workers, the creators of the plan knew clearly that such new communities must be set free to craft their own future in the interest of mission to Hispanic persons.

The Rediscovery of the Primacy of the Local Church

The United Methodist Church, in its present form, is one of the most hierarchical, bureaucratic churches in Christendom. While critics of decentralization cringe at this sort of talk, charging that we are in danger of creeping "congregationalism," we believe that our church must decentralize and accentuate the local congregation as the basic unit of the church.

Now is the time to ask ourselves what new thing God may be doing among us in the present age. When increasing numbers of our congregations are finding helpful resources outside the bounds of those produced by the denomination, when pastors of our largest congregations ignore the connectional structures and create interdenominational parachurch mission organizations, when ethnic minority congregations find that they have more in common with similar ethnic congregations of other denominations than with churches within their own connection, we are seeing the first signs of decentralization within our own church. This decentralization we interpret to be not a sign of decline or infidelity to Christian mission but rather a sign of a new sense of mission and empowerment at the local church level. Put bluntly, *if we deny decentralization and the primacy of the local congregation, our congregations will continue to weaken, our mission and outreach funds will continue to shrink, and The United Methodist Church will die. If we affirm decentralization and local congregations, we will prosper.*

The Primacy of the Local Church and Its Mission

We can now say, with a growing sense of conviction, that a major reason for our denomination's decades of decline is an unstated, but nevertheless real, prejudice against the local church. When our *Discipline* speaks of a congregation as "the local church," it does so in order to indicate that here, in this gathered congregation, is the church, but not the whole church. This local congregation participates in that great universal reality called the church. Our connectionalism is our United Methodist attempt to embody the unity in and participation with the universal church. Yet our polity has moved from this noble insight to structures that are detrimental to the mission of the local congregation and the connection as a whole. Our glorification of our "connectionalism" and our inbred prejudice against the weaknesses of "congregationalism" must not blind us to the weaknesses within connectionalism, *as it has developed in the past three decades.*

We stress connectionalism within the past decades in order to indicate that the structures of connectionalism as most of us know it are a far cry from connectionalism as experienced during the greater part of the history of our church. In our *Discipline*, connectionalism is never linked to our current structure. Rather, we are connected by vision, memory, community, discipline, and leadership. Our denomination, as a denomination, existed for most of its life as a national meeting every four years, with a few committees that encouraged denominational efforts in areas like publishing, evangelism, and mission. For our first one hundred and fifty years, the only connecting agency was the publishing house.

Beginning in about the early twentieth century, our national bureaucracy began to grow. A complex system of manatory taxation, the present apportionment system, was developed. Apportionments began in 1918 as a way to assist the giving of local congregations. Then, the general church, along with a burgeoning national church, along with a burgeoning annual conference and jurisdictional conference bureaucracy, began demanding more funds and funding became mandatory. In 1980, General Conference went so far as to deny congregations the right to vote on apportionments (*Discipline*, ¶ 712.1). Unfortunately, our general polity appears to be based upon the unstated, but nevertheless pervasive, assumption that "you can't trust the local congregations." Local congregations must be compelled, through complex legislative coercion, to do the right thing or the right thing will not be done.

We believe that our connection must learn again to trust the people in local churches. Trust the laity. Trust parish pastors. There is no future for a church that organizes itself around distrust and coercion of local churches. Symptomatic of this attitude is the response of a pastor, now an Associate General Secretary of one of our agencies, upon hearing our proposals for reform: "You simply can't trust laity. They are too selfish and self-centered. We have to force them to give to anything." We disagree.

We have therefore decided that the earlier attempt at reform, voiced in *Rekindling the Flame* and a number of other books of that era, failed to go far enough:

Revitalization can come only if enough lay members who have no vested interest in the denominational hierarchy and bureaucracy and enough ministers who are willing to risk their minimal vested interest take the necessary bold actions. We already have the structure and the means to change what needs to be changed.[2]

But we now know that the roots of our own denial run much deeper. No matter how many lay leaders rise up and call for change, no matter how many clergy speak out for renewal, renewal cannot occur within the presently mandated structures. The rules and the keepers of the rules are too self-protective. Not only our clergy leaders but our lay leaders as well who vote at General Conference, tend to be too enmeshed in the present order to conceive of a new order. While the legislative changes that we will propose as necessary are not many in number, they are fundamental in nature. In this book we name the specific legislative changes that must be made if local United Methodist churches are to be strengthened in their mission. There is a way forward, but that way takes more than good intentions. It will take a few, but nevertheless far-reaching, changes in our structure.

Fortunately, there is a great reservoir of talent and vitality among our local congregations. In order to open up the riches God has given us within the local congregation, the people must be trusted. A pastor who attempts to accomplish through coercion or the invocation of rules and paragraphs from the *Discipline* that which can only be accomplished by persuasion and conversion, is soon a pastor without a congregation. Unfortunately, at the top of our denomination, there is the illusion that decisions can be made without regard to the will of the local congregations. Loyalty to the institution in its present form, rather than loyalty to the people who make up the institution, is the reigning mode of operation.

A new imagination for tomorrow's church will arise by God's grace from the creativity and vitality of congregations who find their life in Christ. The local church truly is the church through whose ministries the reign of God must be made known if we expect that reign to be known anywhere. Worshiping, witnessing, serving communities of faithful disciples are Christ's living body in the world. United in one Spirit, bound together in a connectional covenant of mission, they are instruments of God's world-encompassing work.

Vital Congregations—Faithful Disciples, 21

We, therefore, believe that the way out of our present malaise lies in a rediscovery of the power of the local church to be in mission. Deep within us, we United Methodists know the story of a church that was born out of John Wesley's Spirit-induced irritation with an established church that was no longer in touch with the masses, a church that cared more for its own privileges and prerogatives than for the mission of Jesus Christ. Our church in its inception can be our church again, if we test all polity, all denominational structures and institutions on the basis of how effectively they enable the local congregation to be in mission.

Chapter 2

EMPOWER THE LOCAL CHURCH

WILL RECALLS HAVING A CONVERSATION a
few years ago with a member of our General Commission
on Religion and Race. We were talking about the rather
disappointing results of the Ethnic Minority Local Church
Fund. While the fund had been spending millions of dollars to address the evils of racism in our church and society,
the actual numbers and percentage of ethnic minority
United Methodists, particularly African American United
Methodists, had continued to decline. We thought it sad
and ironic that, after the work of our Ethnic Minority
Local Church Fund, we would have fewer African Americans participating in our church than when we began.
Why?

We must have representation from all parts of the Christian family. It is right, in the church, to be guided by divergent
voices who speak for Christ. We asked the person in charge
of the effort why more African American congregations were
not thriving. Her answer in a nutshell was this: African
American congregations would be vital if The United
Methodist Church had more African American bishops.

This is the sort of thinking—all answers flow from the top down—that is killing us. Can one imagine an African American family saying to itself, "We ought to look for a church home. Let's go to a United Methodist church. We hear that many of their bishops are African Americans."

No family, of any ethnic background, thinks like that. Today, with the percentage of African American bishops far greater than the percentage of African American members in our denomination (4 percent), we continue to withdraw from the needs and the gifts of African Americans. We have tried to solve at the top, through the election of more African American bishops and through the goal (which functions as a quota) that 30 percent of all general agency board members must be members of an ethnic minority, problems that must be solved within local congregations.

From what we observe, African American Christians have much in common with Christians in any ethnic group: they first visit a local congregation. If there is capable pastoral leadership, if the Holy Spirit appears to be active in the life of the congregation, if there is vibrant and engaging worship, they visit again. If not, they go elsewhere.

During the same period in which we tried to solve at the top those problems with our racism in the local congregations, something fascinating was occurring among our Korean American congregations. Without substantial general church funds, with a minimum of general church interference, local Korean American United Methodist congregations were doubling in size every few years. The 1984 proposal to double our church's size came from a Korean American pastor who saw that this was already happening in Korean American churches. Why was this happening? Pastors were filled with the spirit and dedicated to sacrificial work, dedicated laity tithed and attended weekly Bible study classes, and congregations continually reached out to newcomers in their communities.

Hope Morgan-Ward, a member of the North Carolina Conference, was appointed to a dying rural congregation outside of Raleigh. During her ministry there, she has led the church in the sale of the original church property, moved the congregation two miles down the road, built a new facility, and now must build again because her congregation has already outgrown its new facilities.

Kirbyjon Caldwell is pastor of Windsor Village United Methodist Church just outside of Houston. When he began as pastor, worship attendance averaged twelve persons. Today over five thousand worship every week. Caldwell attributes this growth to strong preaching, excellent music, and commitment to community mission. In a recent interview, as he reviewed this predominantly African American congregation's growth, not once did he mention the larger church as playing a helping role.

Clearly, The United Methodist Church is blessed with capable leaders in our local rural and ethnic churches. And clearly, it is at this local level that growth will take place. Most United Methodists live and die as United Methodists without ever seeing one of our bishops, without ever having direct contact with the staff of one of our general boards or agencies. Most of the solutions to what ails us are to be found within the local congregation. Sadly, we would rather have slogans about racial justice than take a hard look at ourselves and ask, "What do we need to do, at the local church level, to make our church more inclusive?" It is easier to elevate a few ethnic minority clergy out of local pastorates, safely tucking them away within the confines of the bureaucracy, than to intensify our efforts at the local church level to create more ethnic minority United Methodists. Presently, we are working against our goal of making a more ethnically inclusive church by distracting some of our most able ethnic minority pastors into thinking that the real business of the church, the sure mark of ministerial success, is a job in the bureaucracy rather than the creation of a thriving congregation.

A major rationale for the decentralization of our church is that it would enable our ethnic minority constituencies better to mobilize to address their specific needs. As one African American leader in our church said to us, "When we, as about 4 percent of the church, must convince the other 96 percent that something needs to be done for African Americans, very little gets done. It is virtually impossible to move so large a denomination to address the specific issues of a particular racial or ethnic constituency."

The largest Hmong (an ethnic group from Southeast Asia) congregation in the world is a United Methodist church in Minnesota. Several years ago, Andy asked, "How large is the congregation?"

"Six hundred," was the response.

"How many come to worship?"

"Six hundred."

This church is now creating the first United Methodist Hmong hymnal themselves because, as one of their pastors said, "We can't wait for the general church to meet our needs."

When everything must flow from the top down to our ethnic minority members, the best our ethnic minority churches can hope for is an occasional dribbling of subsidies, a few positions set aside within the bureaucracy, a few bishops, more slogans and posturing. The past two decades have demonstrated the ineffectiveness of such centralized efforts. If our church is to greet the rapid expansion of ethnic minority population in the United States with the challenge of the gospel of Jesus Christ, decentralization, in which power is given back to the local congregation, is essential. Decentralization by means of establishing house congregations was the main virtue of the National Plan for Hispanic Ministries.

Creating the Vision

The local church, the congregation gathered to worship and serve God, is the font from which flows much Christian good. We would define the mission of the church from the local congregation outward: *to receive, nurture, equip, and send forth disciples of Jesus Christ.* In our vision, the church beyond the local church—our denomination in its annual, jurisdictional, and General Conference manifestations—exists to help the local church fulfill its mission. Power flows from the "bottom up." The local congregation is not a branch office for the national denomination, not a franchise outlet for denominational programs. The local church is the reason for The United Methodist Church, not vice versa.

This view appeared to be endorsed in the 1990 paper of the Council of Bishops, *Vital Congregations—Faithful Disciples.* There, our bishops said that our local congregations must focus on their communities and the needs of their congregations. Alas, while that 1990 paper was a step in the right direction, it was still too full of sloganeering, with no ideas for needed structural change. It was a step in the right direction, but not as bold a step as we needed. The bishops did not introduce or enact any specific changes in our current system to make their vision possible. That is why we must not merely assert, as did our bishops then, that the local church is important. We must change our structure in order to match our form and function with our vision. The more recent "Vision 2000" program of the General Board of Discipleship does an admirable job of energizing and undergirding the local congregation in its evangelism efforts. Yet such programs, without the necessary structural changes within our polity, will only produce disillusionment and growing cynicism from those who sincerely try to revitalize their local congregation.

Our particular polity has a way of distracting pastors from their main task of upbuilding and edifying the congregation. A new pastor quickly gets the impression that professional advancements often appears to be based on factors other than an assessment of that pastor's effectiveness in the local church. Loyalty to the system at large, relationships with ministerial peers, an ability "to deliver" apportionments, a basic unwillingness to rock the ark are more valued by cabinets and bishops making appointments than a clear assessment of that pastor's ability to help the local church accomplish its mission. A pastor's effectiveness in leading a local congregation should be the basis of pastoral promotion.

> **¶ 245.2: The pastor shall be the chief administrative officer of the local church and charge and shall be a member of the Charge Conference and an ex-officio member (with vote) of all boards, councils, commissions, committees, and task forces elected or appointed in the church/ charge, except as otherwise provided by the *Discipline*.**

There has also been a tendency in recent decades to think of the *real* work of the church as being anywhere other than within the local congregation. Mission is what happens elsewhere, something coordinated by someone at the head office in New York. Christian education occurs when one has skillfully used those official resources produced by someone in Nashville. Good worship happens when one follows the proper rituals as devised by a general church committee. Justice for women will come when every conference, district, and church follows the guidelines handed down by the General Commission on the Status and Role of Women.

> My beginning point is the local congregation. This is
> not to even remotely suggest that congregationalism
> is being advocated. Rather, connectionalism will be
> greatly strengthened as local churches grow stronger.
> Healthy congregations equal healthy connection.
> Many local congregations in my annual conference
> have lost their way. They are unsure about who they
> are, what they are supposed to be about and where to
> find help.
>
> *Dolores B. Queen, District Superintendent,*
> *Western North Carolina Conference*

One of us recalls hearing a district superintendent scolding a charge conference because, "Nearly three-fourths of your expenditures are for yourselves, your pastor's salary and her benefits package." The superintendent's point was that true mission necessitates sending the congregation's money elsewhere. The *Discipline* states that the paying of apportionments "is the first benevolent responsibility" of each congregation. Yet what happens to the money sent elsewhere? The vast majority of funds sent to annual conference and to general agencies and funds go to pay someone's salary. Why is it more missional to pay someone's salary in Nashville, Nairobi, or New York than to pay a pastor's salary in Springfield?

We have become victims of the line of reason that thinks the most important work of God is always elsewhere, beyond the local setting. So "prophetic" action involves the General Conference making pronouncements to Congress, or establishing "Shalom Zones" in Los Angeles. Mission means big statements and large programs in which money flows from the local congregation to the top, then the mission may trickle back down to the local level.

Let's be honest. There is something quite enticing in the notion that the *real* ministry of the church is elsewhere, somewhere other than the local congregation. Life in the local church can be tough. There, things are done face-to-face. There, the local people have a keen sense of ownership; they expect to have a say in policy and to oversee and evaluate what is actually accomplished. Any pastor can testify that it is often easier to send money to do good work in Africa than to mobilize the local congregation to work in its own neighborhood. Many of our United Methodist congregations find themselves in situations in which they do not have to look far for work of Christ to do. Social disintegration, the breakup of families, and the crisis of our youth are problems on our own doorstep. Yet to address those problems would require local courage, and local conversion, and local vision. So it can be easier to keep things global.

By decentralizing our church, we can empower local congregations to mobilize to address their pressing needs and the needs of their communities. We are thinking now of the pastor in West Virginia who told us of waiting for two years for a representative from the General Board of Global Ministries to come to his church to speak on world mission. A group in his church had felt the call of God to take their skills in carpentry, plumbing, and building construction to some place of need in the developing world. Finally, the representative arrived one Sunday, in a very expensive rental car, dressed in finery to which this little congregation was unaccustomed, and managed to alienate most of the congregation with a condescending attitude toward them.

After a frustrating twelve months of unreturned telephone calls, red tape, and runaround, the pastor in West Virginia called a pastor in the Caribbean, made the necessary arrangements, and a mission team was dispatched to help build a community clinic. Since that time, this church has sent annual teams of plumbers, carpenters, bricklayers, and others to some area of need. We believe this is the model for the future.

Korean United Methodist churches, the fastest growing ethnic segment in our connection, recently demonstrated that they need one another more than they need the connection. These congregations have learned to share resources and ideas for ministry with one another that may not be relevant to the larger denomination, but which have proved to be essential for Korean United Methodists. The recent proposal to create a Korean Missionary Conference within the United States testifies to the frustration that many of these congregations are feeling within annual conferences that may not understand their needs. These congregations may not need their annual conferences, but their annual conferences certainly need them.

What Should Be Done?

Local congregations will become the center of the United Methodist system by implementing five specific changes, four of which require disciplinary action. These changes will allow each local congregation to (1) define its own mission, (2) create its own structure, (3) voluntarily support apportioned funds, (4) pay the full cost of pastoral leadership, and (5) give the congregation a greater voice in selecting the pastor it needs.

1. Encourage Local Congregations to Define Their Mission

We must begin by encouraging each congregation to define its own ministry and mission in its own particular setting. While this is now allowed and encouraged, we have not taken the next steps of letting local congregations follow through on their decisions.

After decades of waiting for the general church or the annual conference to decide what real mission is, each local church must now struggle with its particular call to ministry and mission. Each congregation ought to have a mission statement to guide its mission, its giving, and its internal structure. This statement of purpose and mission should be a concise picture of where this congregation intends to go in its life together. It should be its theological guide and benchmark in congregational planning, budgeting, and mission. When the time comes for a change in pastoral leadership, that statement of mission, along with consultation between the cabinet and the leaders of the congregation, should determine the choice of pastor.

An Alternative to Our Present Planning

For a number of years I have felt something was wrong with how local churches are doing long-range planning. If we are to be the Body of Christ, if Jesus is to be our head of the church, then it makes sense that our planning of the church's ministries should reflect the guidance of God, that we should do what God wants. I said to my congregation that it does not matter what I think we should do as a church, even though I am the pastor; it does not matter what any one of the members of the church thinks we should do as a church. It is what Christ thinks that should mold and shape who we are and what we do as the church of Jesus Christ.

Out of this tension between our practice and who we are called to be by being followers of Christ, I decided to try a new approach. The irony is that nothing is new about this approach, it is just ordering our life and decisions and ministries around the guidance of God through the work of the Holy Spirit just as the church did in Acts. What is pathetic is that something so basic to our identity as Christians comes across as novel!

We set three Sunday nights aside for an all church meeting. One guideline was that if you were going to participate in the final evening of deciding what the church would do in its ministries for the future, you had to attend the preceding sessions of biblical studies and prayer. The first night we only studied the scriptures. We spent the whole evening reading New Testament texts to hear what the Bible had to say as to who we are as the church. What is the essence of the church, what does it mean to be the church, what does the church do as the church, what characteristics does the church of Jesus Christ have. We looked at the things Jesus said and did. We spent time looking at the ministries of the New Testament church as reported in Acts, Paul's writings, and others. It was a great evening with many people exclaiming that they had never heard all that the Bible said about the church in one setting. It helped them see the big picture of biblical direction as to what the church is.

On our second evening we gathered in the church sanctuary for two hours of prayer. First we reviewed the biblical understanding of the nature of the church. Next we spread out around the sanctuary, gave away our concerns to God's keeping for the next 120 minutes. Then I read a combination of biblical texts and pertinent significant Christian writings about aspects of who we are as the church, the Body of Christ. Five minutes of silence followed each reading for prayer and meditation as to what God wanted our church to do in its ministries in Homer, Alaska. During the silence I the pastor prayed for each individual that was present trying to discern God's will for our church. We closed with a group prayer in a circle around the altar. We all felt we had been on holy ground that evening.

The third week we gathered to review the biblical guidance as to the nature of the church and its ministries, share what promptings of the Holy Spirit we had received in our times of prayer, and to ask the question, "Where is all this leading us?" First we made a list of all the aspects of our church that were in line with our understanding of what it means to be the church. Next we compared the list of all the aspects and ministries of our church that presently reflect Christ as the head of the church with the list of information we gleaned from our time of biblical study and prayer. We made a list of ministries of the church that we were presently not doing that are in line with God's call to us as God's church, and asked the question, "What would it mean for our church to move out into the deeper water and cast our nets into the sea of the world? Where might Jesus be calling our church into specific ministries in our church community, the community we live in, and our world?" We ran out of time and scheduled a fourth meeting two weeks later to finish our task and to answer the question, not of what we think we should be doing as the church, but given the Bible, our time in prayer, the needs of our community and world, our church's talents, gifts, and our unique place in time, where is God calling us to be in ministry?

This is the most faithful experience of trying to order our church and our life as the church in accordance with God's will that I have ever been a part of.

The Reverend Steven Lambert
Homer, Alaska

We predict a great groundswell of divinely inspired energy and creativity emanating from our congregations—if we have the courage and the vision to get out of the way and allow the Holy Spirit to work among us and our congregations.

2. Reform the Organizational Structure of Congregations

Most of the current *Discipline*'s mandated structure for the local congregation is unnecessary, a function not of a process of a congregation's assessment of its own mission but of the general church's mistrust of its congregations to form themselves. In recent years, various boards and agencies, as well as some caucus groups, have used the *Discipline*'s paragraphs on the organization of the local church to force their own agendas upon the local congregation. They have mandated various committees and observances, assorted chairpersons of this or that.

While serving in Nashville, Andy had the opportunity to impose such structure throughout the connection. Andy wrote, encouraged, and passed disciplinary legislation that mandated an annual conference worship area with specific responsibilities, and a local church chairperson of worship with four long paragraphs of specific responsibilities. Faithful to his office as administrator of worship in the denomination, he mandated that everyone else follow his agenda. But did these actions really serve any local congregation? Possibly, but probably not.

Why does each local church have its internal organization determined by the General Conference? A certain amount of uniformity is important in a connectional system like United Methodism. *We propose that every church should retain a charge conference, trustees, a committee on nominations, a finance committee, a pastor-parish relations committee, and a significantly reconfigured church council.* These will provide for the essential ministries of property and leadership. United Methodist Men and Women and a lay leader also remain. All else is optional, related to that church's vision of its ministry.

¶ 253: ~~1.~~ The ~~Administrative~~ **Church** Council shall provide for the planning and implementing of a program of nurture, outreach, witness, and resources in the local church, and for the administration of its organizational and temporal life. ~~The Administrative Council shall have all of the responsibilities of the Administrative Board (257) and the Council on Ministries (258), including evaluation, setting of goals, and developing strategies and plans of action for implementing its ministries.~~ The ~~Administrative~~ **Church** Council shall be amenable to and function as the executive agency of the Charge Conference (¶ 248). Its membership shall include the ~~combined membership of those named to the Administrative Board and the Council on Ministries insofar as the officers, or combination of offices, listed in 255 and 259 exist within the local church or are otherwise provided for in this paragraph.~~ **chairperson of the Church Council; the pastor(s); the lay leader; the lay member(s) of the Annual Conference; the chairperson of the Committee on Finance; the chairperson (or representative, if the chairperson is from another church on a multi-church charge) of the Committee on Pastor-Parish Relations; the chairperson of the Board of Trustees; representatives of the nurturing, outreach, and witness ministries of the church; and such other persons as the Charge Conference may determine. The employed professional staff who are members of the Church Council shall not vote on matters pertaining to their employee relationship.**

A few decades ago, general church consistency was achieved by a relatively lean local church organization with a few committees and a simple board structure. The rest was left to the individual congregation. Several committees were mentioned by the *Discipline*, but these were organized only if needed. Congregations with a large number of members, a large and complex budget, and many congregational programs were free to be as complex in their internal organization as needed.

Today, the *Discipline* has clearly taken the larger congregation as its norm. There are too many committees and the structure is too complex, expending too much of the congregation's energy in finding people to fill the mandated positions. One of the most debilitating organizational moves came in 1968 when the General Conference attempted to effect the union of two church families—the Evangelical United Brethren and the Methodists—by combining the local church structure of each into a mandated structure, parallel to our general church structure, for every United Methodist congregation. For over a decade, United Methodist congregations, large and small, struggled with a complex council on ministries combined with a redundant administrative board. In 1980, the General Conference allowed smaller congregations to simplify their structure—but only with the prior approval from the district superintendent.

Because there is an attempt in the present structure to relate the work of each unit in the local church to every other unit, some people (such as the lay leader), by virtue of their office, serve on many committees and boards. Therefore some of our officers find themselves attending many meetings and expending energy in these meetings which ought to be used in action.

Because there is an attempt to involve the maximum number of persons in the decision-making process, decisions come slowly and church officers find themselves in protracted discussions of too many internal issues. The present structure gives congregational leaders the impression that the main task of a congregational leaders is to attend meetings focused entirely upon the internal maintenance of the congregation. Few laypersons can be found with great enthusiasm for the expenditure of large amounts of their time in mere administration of a congregation. Rather than actual involvement in the tasks of mission, evangelism, worship, and service, our presently mandated congregational structure demands far too much time for internal maintenance.

> You can always tell a failing business by the number of meetings it has. When a business is failing, and its leaders do not know what to do, they have meetings where everyone can look at each other and blame one another rather than do what successful businesses do—go out and find customers.
>
> *A United Methodist businessperson from Ohio*

We believe that each congregation must be free to organize itself, as much as is possible, on the basis of its own congregational culture, its own vision of its mission, and its most natural style of decision making, congregational involvement, and leadership. Such permission is already given to congregations related to the central conferences outside the United States. Now is the time to bring this missional vision to the church within the United States.

¶ 253.2-4: Delete these sections (have to do with various mandates related to Administrative Council).
¶¶ 254-257: Delete these paragraphs (have to do with Administrative Board).

¶¶ **258-259:** Delete these paragraphs (have to do with Council on Ministries).

¶¶ **260-263:** Delete these paragraphs (have to do with coordinators, work areas, program support personnel).

¶ **264:** Delete §§ 3-5, and 7 (have to do with ministries with young adults, singles, and older adults; and prison ministry).

The current *Discipline* forces a bureaucratic, corporate America (alas, corporate America of 1960!) style of organization which is not only now outmoded but also unfair to the diversity within United Methodism. A congregation does not make decisions the way a large corporation makes decisions. In the congregation, we learn to trust the wisdom of the congregation's saints rather than mere majority vote. People have power within the congregation, not on the basis of where their name fits on some corporate organizational flowchart, but rather on the basis of the trust their fellow members have in them and their decisions.

Again, our current mandated local church structure appears to be based on two disastrous assumptions: (1) You can't trust the local church, and (2) The purpose of the local church is to serve the general church. Our form is killing our spirit. Aside from a few basic guidelines and organizing principles, each local church needs to be free to organize itself in ways that are most appropriate to that congregation's mission. What would happen if congregations were left to determine how they would witness and minister? It is likely that issues of importance in the local church and community would be addressed. Whatever happened would be done because the people felt it was

¶ 245. The basic organizational plan for the local church shall include provision for the following units: a Charge Conference, ~~an Administrative~~ a **Church** Council ~~or Administrative Board and Council on Ministries~~, a Committee on Pastor-Parish Relations, a Board of Trustees, a Committee on Finance, a Committee on Nominations and Personnel, and such other elected leaders, commissions, councils, committees, and task forces as the Charge Conference may determine. Every local church shall ~~choose~~ **develop** a plan for organizing its administrative and programmatic responsibilities. **It is intended that each local congregation provide a comprehensive program of nurture, outreach, and witness, along with the planning and administration of the congregation's organizational and temporal life.**

important. The people would have a high sense of ownership for the church program. Detailed, patronizing legislation from on high is a shortcut for convincing people that certain needs ought to be met, an attempt by the general church to achieve through the law what only the gospel can do. We must trust the power of the gospel to create, at the local church level, the sort of church the gospel demands.

3. Voluntary Support of Apportionments

Our denomination, like many other contemporary institutions, appears to be organized around the principle that the people cannot be trusted. The institution assumes that it must force the people, through a variety of means, to support the institution, in ways determined by the institution, or support will not be forthcoming. We are in a time of widespread distrust of large institutions in which large institutions are learning that it is they who must earn the trust of the people, not the people who must prove themselves to the institution. Consider recent United States political elections in which candidates have run as individuals, against the Washington establishment, against even their own political parties. And they have won. Consider the numerous American businesses that are developing new ways of listening to and responding to the needs of their customers. According to the 1994 survey by the General Council on Ministries, 60 percent of annual conference delegates believe that the local congregation must have "more say in apportionments."

If . . . The United Methodist Church were to adopt funding only the Episcopal and District Superintendent Funds, and World Service, but no other general, jurisdictional, conference, or district funds, we would have $60,000 in my local church for programming, mission, and growth! Multiply that figure by our conference's top twenty-five churches and you have already funneled more than $1.5 million back into those twenty-five local church budgets.

A pastor in North Carolina

We are now emboldened to say that each of our charge conferences must have the option to decide whether or not to support financially the ministries of the connection, based upon that congregation's perceived value of the services rendered.

Allowing voluntary support of apportionments may be accomplished by changes to just a few paragraphs of the

¶ **248.14:** . . . what amounts have been apportioned to it for ~~World Service and Conference Benevolences~~ **general church and Annual Conference program agencies and causes** . . . the importance of ~~World Service and Conference Benevolences~~ **these apportionments.** . . . ~~The World Service Fund is basic in the financial program of The United Methodist Church. World Service on apportionment represents the minimum needs for the mission and ministry of the Church.~~ Payment ~~in full~~ of these apportionments ~~by local churches~~ is **one of** the ~~first~~ benevolent ~~responsibility~~ **responsibilities** of the Church ~~(¶ 912)~~. **Each Charge Conference shall have the right to revise the apportionment for each general agency, council, commission, and fund requested by the General Conference, except the Episcopal Fund and the funds for conducting General Conference; each apportionment from the jurisdiction; each apportionment from the Annual Conference, except the District Superintendents' Fund, pension and benefits funds for pre-1982 service, the Equitable Compensation Fund, and the costs of Annual Conference meeting; and each apportionment from the district.** The district superintendent or designated agent shall also notify . . . .

Discipline. First, rather than requiring apportionments, we suggest changing the *Discipline* to read: "Payment of these apportionments is one of the benevolent responsibilities of the church. Each charge conference shall vote on the apportionment requested from each general agency and fund, each apportionment from the jurisdiction, each apportionment from the annual conference, and each apportionment from the district." The current system insists that the majority of all funds be considered as "block apportionments" (such as the majority of our general agencies, plus other funds that are considered as one, along with conference apportionments, as one line item: "World Service"). Our proposal allows each congregation to accept, reject, or revise most apportioned funds.

To make this possible, the World Service Fund must be broken up as a block fund and uncoupled from conference benevolences. We recommend that the *Discipline* be changed to delete any reference to a unified World Service Fund. Rather than combining the general agency budgets into one, let each general agency, commission, and council be a separate line item. At the same time, allow each annual conference to accept, reject, or revise the general apportioned funds with or without reduction throughout a quadrennium, as well as allow conference benevolences to be considered by local congregations separately.

¶ **711.3:** d) (Becomes ¶ 711.4, with remaining sections renumbered) **4.** *General Church Funds:* d) The council, on receiving from the treasurer of the General Council on Finance and Administration a statement of the amounts apportioned that Annual Conference for ~~World Service~~ **general church funds for the support of general agencies, councils, and commissions,** shall ~~combine the total World Service apportionment, without reduction for the quadrennium, and the approved conference benevolences budget (¶ 711.3a). The sum of these two amounts shall be known as World Service and Conference Benevolences. The World Service and Conference Benevolences budget thus established shall include a~~

~~statement of the percentage for World Service and the percentage for conference benevolences." (See also ¶ 712.)~~ recommend to the Annual Conference the amount of each such apportionment which the Annual Conference will accept for apportionment to the local churches, with the exception of the Episcopal Fund and funds for conducting the General Conference, which shall be apportioned without reduction, and the Annual Conference shall act to adopt or amend those recommendations as a part of the business of its annual session. These apportionments shall not be combined together, nor shall they be combined with conference benevolences in the apportionments to local congregations.

This is not as radical as it may sound. Most people still have a basic tendency to support institutions where they are members. Yet no segment of the church should any longer assume, simply because it has achieved the status of a line item in the apportionments, that it need no longer interpret itself and its work to the congregations. At present, charge conferences are simply told by the annual conference, which is told by the general church, what their apportionments are. Of course, many congregations are electing not to pay their "required" apportionments, and thousands of individual United Methodists are simply giving less or giving elsewhere in silent protest. According to the General Council on Finance and Administration's annual report for 1994, 15 percent of the monies requested were simply not received. Surely a message is being sent that calls for a reassessment of this system.

Our General Conference continues blindly approving

budgets that have no chance under the present system of being fully funded. We believe that each charge conference ought to have the opportunity to decide whether or not to pay for the funds of the connectional church. Rather than lump general agencies and funds under a general fund such as World Service, the connection ought to show congregations what they are paying for in the work of the General Board of Global Ministries, the General Board of Discipleship, and the other agencies that huddle together. Rather than hide staff costs under the innocuous (and possibly misleading) label of "conference benevolences," the annual conference ought to ask congregations for specific support of the salaries and expenses of conference staff, as well as the costs of conference missions and programs. This will not only make our various agencies more responsive to the local church, but it will also give local congregations an enhanced sense of responsibility for the programs of the connection.

In southern Florida, a predominantly Anglo congregation of our acquaintance has chosen not to pay its full apportionments, electing instead to spend some of its mission dollars to create two new storefront churches, one in a predominantly African American neighborhood and another in a Hispanic neighborhood. We predict that increasing numbers of our congregations will become convinced that their methods of meeting local social and religious needs are much more cost-effective than those employed by the general church. This realization may lead to a great dismantling of the general denominational benevolence and missional structure unless that structure takes immediate steps to connect the local church to itself, not by more legislation or mandates, but rather by better communication and responsiveness to the local church. Local people must feel that they are joining voluntarily with our national and global mission and benevolent efforts, or those efforts will continue to be plagued by radically shrinking support.

Admittedly, this new, noncoercive funding may force the larger connection into asking some tough questions about the cost-effectiveness and missional value of many of our programs and agencies. It's time for tough questions. For example, for several years, the Native American Awareness Sunday spent more for publicity than the special offering raised. Did this serve the cause of Native American United Methodists? One layperson said, "At General Conference, invariably some of those who speak out in defense of required apportionments and continued increases in our budget are those whose churches fall far short of paying their full apportionments. It's hypocritical of them to defend a system which they and their churches have shown their unwillingness or inability to fund."

Declining revenues will force us into major cutbacks and reorganization. We fear that, in the present structure, too many of those retrenchment decisions are going to be made by those at the top, who are protecting what turf they can, salvaging the status quo to the best of their ability, rather than listening to the will of the local congregations and making changes on the basis of the local congregations' commitment to the ministries of the connection.

The major fear persons have expressed about our proposals is that designated giving will cause necessary ministries to suffer. We disagree and offer the United Way as proof. In the past several years, because of a variety of factors, giving to the unified budget of the United Way began to fall. In response, the United Way began to allow individuals to give to the whole or to give to specific programs (Boy Scouts, Planned Parenthood, or whatever program the individual chose). Giving increased to the specific programs and to the unified budget. Our own general church's Section on Stewardship has wondered aloud if the days of any unified budgets (from the local church budgets to the general church budgets) are nearing an end. Does anyone doubt that more money will be given to missions if congregations are allowed to support and be in dialogue with specific missionaries versus the current system of supporting 644 nameless, faceless missionaries through a unified budget?

4. Paying for Pastoral Ministry

Emphasizing the local congregation will be a great challenge for many of our more dependent, less-engaged congregations. Our present system has fostered a sense of institutional dependency on the part of some of our churches. In *Rekindling the Flame*, Bob Wilson estimated that 70 percent of our congregations (typically our smaller churches) are subsidized in some way by the larger connection. These subsidies include grants for facilities, but most consist of subsidies for clergy. Salaries, health insurance, and pensions are subsidized for well over half of all our clergy. The main purpose of these subsidies is not to support the mission of the church but rather to preserve our leaders from having to make tough decisions about congregations that no longer have a mission, and to aid the clergy guild in protecting one another.

¶ **722.** *Equitable Compensation.*—2. It is the purpose of the Commission on Equitable Compensation to support ordained ministry in the charges of the Annual Conference by (1) recommending conference standards for clergy support; (2) administering funds to be used ~~in~~ **for** base compensation supplementation **in missional support situations, including a determination, in regular consultation with the Cabinet, of the appointments in the conference which** are to be so designated; and (3) providing counsel and advisory material on clergy support to district superintendents and Committees on Pastor-Parish Relations.

¶ 722.3: The commission shall carefully study the needs for additional support **in missional support situations** within the conference and the sources of income, and shall recommend annually to the conference for its action a schedule of minimum base compensation for all full-time ~~pastors or those clergy members of the Annual Conference appointed~~ and less than full-time **pastors serving** ~~to a local church~~ **such appointments** . . . .

¶ 722.6: In consultation with the Commission on Equitable Compensation, the Council on Finance and Administration shall recommend to the conference its estimate of the amount required to support the schedule of minimum base compensation and base compensation supplements for ~~the~~ pastors **serving missional support appointments,** as adopted by the conference.

¶ 722.8: The Equitable Compensation Fund . . . shall be used to provide each pastor **serving a missional support appointment** who receives less than the minimum . . . . no member in good standing who is appointed to a pastoral charge **defined as a missional support appointment** is denied the minimum base compensation.

Our church, which ought to have one of the most flexible and adaptable means of clergy deployment, has developed a rigid, poorly adapted system whereby unproductive clergy can be subsidized, and ineffective congregations can be preserved from tough choices through minimum salary subsidies for clergy salary, pensions, and insurance.

Therefore, we think it is essential that *each congregation be wholly responsible for its pastoral ministry.* By requiring that local congregations be responsible for the total compensation of pastoral staff, we would enable each congregation to receive exactly the amount of leadership for which the congregation is willing and able to pay. In the early days of this century, a presiding elder could apply to the annual conference or General Board of Missions for help with clergy salary support in a mission situation. In the late 1930s, minimum salary—the program that would enable every Methodist pastor to work at a fair wage—was developed. (The federal government initiated the minimum wage in 1938.) The program continues today, even though the missional rationale for minimum slary has been lost, transformed into a sort of guaranteed minimum wage for all clergy.

Minimum salary has had a number of debilitating effects. Rather than being a "floor" for clergy salaries, minimum salary has all too often functioned as an artificial "ceiling." According to *Rekindling the Flame,* in many annual conferences, 40 to 50 percent of all the pastors' cash salaries tend to cluster around the required minimum salary level. Minimum salary may actually depress clergy income by making a low level of compensation seem more rational than it really is.

Perhaps more detrimental to the life of the local church, minimum salary protects our district superintendents and our congregational leaders from having to make tough decisions about congregations that may have had a great mission in years past but not today. We therefore spend most of our resources propping up congregations and their buildings from yesterday while lacking the funds to reach out to today's needs. For every new church we build in a new neighborhood, we are keeping hundreds of churches open in neighborhoods that no longer need so many redundant United Methodist churches.

Most detrimental of all, the minimum salary program tends to shift responsibility for ministerial support away from the local congregation to the denomination. Although all funds for minimum salary come from the collection plates of individual congregations, naturally pastors on minimum salary tend to see the annual conference, rather than the congregation, as their employer. Under minimum salary, both pastor and congregation develop a dependent, passive relationship with the annual conference.

We propose that there be no denominational subsidies for any congregation—including subsidies for salary, pensions, and insurance—except for definite, missional reasons. These subsidies must be reviewed and evaluated annually on the basis of specific missional objectives. At present, it is difficult for our church to send a pastor into a deteriorated, inner-city situation to form a United Methodist mission in a neighborhood which, without external subsidy, would have no ministry. We are hindered from such bold mission because we are too preoccupied keeping afloat pastors who are only marginally needed in congregations that no longer have a viable mission.

In order to mobilize for mission within the local church, and to end the complex, expensive, and debilitating subsidy system, we must search for more creative means of clergy remuneration. Our present system needs to be more supportive of clergy who want to engage in "tent making" ministry (working part time in one job while serving a church), and of two clergy persons who wish to share time and salary in one church.

In the past decades our system has encouraged a lamentable professionalization of the pastoral vocation. This is ironic in a movement that began as a gathering of Wesley's *lay* preachers. We have many clergy who are not only underpaid but also underemployed in congregations that are too small to need the services of a full-time pastor. Too often we have placed full-time pastors in churches where their full-time efforts have (unintentionally) robbed the laity of their God-given ministry. If the small congregation is struggling (with denominational subsidies, of course) to pay a full-time pastor to visit the sick, to recruit new members, to teach and to plan worship, why should any of the laity assume these responsibilities? More part-time clergy could lead to a much needed recovery of the many valid ministries of the laity.

The proportion of United Methodist expenditures needed to support the clergy has been steadily increasing. In 1970, the church spent 28 percent of all money on ministerial support; in 1984 the proportion was 31.7 percent, and in 1990 it was 32.6 percent, an increase in actual dollars from $315.5 million in 1973 to $948.5 million in 1990. It is time to reverse this trend.

Denominational leaders have claimed that full-time, seminary trained, professional clergy are more effective. Is that demonstrably true? It is our impression that a comparison of the number of members received on profession of faith by our nonseminary trained local pastors with the numbers received by our seminary trained pastors, for example, does not demonstrate that seminaries are the only place to train practitioners of evangelism!

Our expensively trained, full-time, professional pastors are incredibly costly to support. One of the reasons why we have a deplorable record of new church beginnings in the past few decades is that it costs our denomination much more to form a financially viable congregation than it costs a denomination that is flexible enough to have part-time and unsubsidized clerical leadership. In addition, the pressure to have all clergy seminary trained and full members of the annual conference is increasing the difficulty of securing pastors in our ethnic congregations.

We suspect that the relatively recent United Methodist penchant for these seminary trained, professional clergy is not that they are more effective but rather that these clergy tend to be more integrated into, more dependent upon, and therefore less critical of the institution to which they are dependent for salary and advancement.

5. Expand Consultation Prior to Appointments

Local congregations, along with their pastors, must have the ability to participate more fully in the appointment system. The United Methodist Church is heir to a unique system of clergy assignment. Each pastor is appointed by the bishop, who has authority "to make and fix the appointments" (1992 *Discipline*, ¶ 516.1). Pastors, at their ordination, enter into a covenant with all the ordained ministers of the annual conference, agreeing to go where the church feels their gifts and graces are best suited to an individual congregation. "They offer themselves without reserve," says the *Discipline* (¶ 421) "to be appointed and to serve, after consultation, as the appointive authority may determine." Because the clergy are appointed by the bishop, with the district superintendents, clergy tend to concern themselves more about the cabinet's perception rather than with their performance as a pastor of a congregation.

Yet this tendency is in tension, in our opinion, with the basic concept of United Methodist clergy deployment: our clergy vow to devote themselves entirely to the spreading of the gospel, giving their ministry in the congregation priority over personal concerns. At ordination, our pastors pledge their willingness to go where the church (in practice, the bishop and the cabinet) feels that the minister's talents can best help the mission of the church. The rationale for The United Methodist Church, as a denomination, must be the mission of the local church. The rationale for ordained clergy must be the mission of the local church. Our system should be a marvelous means of energetically deploying clergy in support of the mission of the church. Alas, other factors often take precedence over this essentially missional means of clergy assignment. For instance, an informal seniority system, not mandated by the *Discipline*, but nevertheless rigidly followed, has developed within the appointments of the annual conference. Clergy are expected to follow a career track which moves them "up the ladder" to larger churches after they have "paid their dues" in the small churches. While there is nothing wrong with allowing less experienced clergy to gain experience in less demanding parishes, and with rewarding those who have served well, the seniority system is an example of the ways in which our church appointment system functions on behalf of the clergy rather than the local church. Again, we cite *Rekindling the Flame:*

> The tragedy of the present seniority system is that it very often results in bad matches of ministers and congregations. When salary level and years of service become the most important factors (alas the *only* factors), ministers are sent to churches in which the skills of the pastor are not appropriate to the needs of the congregation. . . . The mission of the church receives less attention than the professional advancement of the minister. Over the long term, neither the clergy nor the congregations are well served by such a system.[1]

The mission of the local church must take precedence over the career advancement of clergy. Our clergy need to see that their advancement, in terms of salary and responsibility, are tied to their performance in the congregations to which they are appointed. For instance, studies have shown that the fifth year is usually the most effective year of a pastor's term in a congregation. Yet our pastors are routinely moved in many conferences after the fourth year. The average length of service in 1994 was still four years. Why? There is no directive on the best timing for clergy moves in our *Discipline*. Last year, in a conference in the Southeast, 87 percent of the churches in the conference that received a new pastor did not request the change. Thirteen percent did request a change, but cabinets asked for a move in 32 percent of the cases, pastors in 47 percent. Eight percent of the moves resulted from a combination of requests. The implication to us is that the pastors or the cabinet initiated the moves believing that this was the best way to enhance the pastors' careers, or to increase salary.

Our district superintendents and bishops need to demonstrate that pastoral effectiveness in helping a congregation fulfill its mission is the main criterion for pastoral appointment in United Methodism. It is not sinful for pastors to desire better salaries. But it must be clear that higher pastoral salaries are tied to the recruitment of more members for the congregation, or increased financial commitment on the part of the members, or increased involvement in mission and outreach, rather than to being merely a loyal servant to the institutional status quo.

Laypeople are often astounded at the lack of knowledge bishops have about their churches and their pastors. To many laypeople, the appointment of pastors is the primary function of the bishop. How could a bishop neglect a function that is so central? In United Methodism, many of our bishops have responsibility for a large number of congregations. Yet it is possible to devise the statistical and other means to obtain an accurate picture of each congregation and each pastor.

> We met—for weeks we met—discussing the needs of our congregation, our hopes and dreams for the future. Out of those discussions, we determined that our major need was for evangelism, new members, growth. We told the bishop that we wanted a pastor who could lead us in evangelism. When our new pastor was appointed, the bishop told me, "I've found the man that you are looking for." That is exactly what he told me.
>
> I had my doubts after my first conversation with our newly appointed minister. Then I looked back in the Conference Journal. This guy had been at his former appointment for five years and, in five years, had received less than ten new members. Some evangelist! Doesn't the bishop have access to the *Conference Journal?*
>
> *A layperson in the Southeastern Jurisdiction*

Most United Methodist congregations rate preaching as the most important task of the pastor. Yet how many district superintendents or bishops ever hear their pastors preach? New ministerial members of the annual conference quickly learn that their advancement and their future will be evaluated by factors other than their preaching ability. The gap between lay expectations for their pastors and the system's evaluation and placement of its pastors grows. The gap must be narrowed. Our district superintendents and our bishops must become more cognizant of and more responsive to the expectations of our laity.

Laypeople, who routinely list "good preaching" as the top attribute in a pastor, cannot understand and should not tolerate the cabinet and bishop routinely appointing pastors to positions without ever once hearing the pastor preach. District superintendents would better use their Sundays visiting in congregations within their district, not *preaching to* the congregation, but rather *listening with* the congregation. With video and audio tapes, there is no excuse for lack of knowledge of a pastor's preaching competence.

Appointment must be made in reference to the missional needs of the congregation, not in primary reference to the salary level or years of service of the pastor. If a bishop is unable to tell a congregation, on the basis of that congregation's statement of mission, why a pastor is appointed to them, then the bishop needs to take a critical look at the pastor. It is not the congregation's responsibility to supply guaranteed employment for incompetent pastors; it is the bishop's responsibility to provide the congregation a competent pastor.

The notion of "guaranteed appointments" is as outmoded and dysfunctional as tenure is for university professors. The justification of such a practice on the basis of an appeal to "freedom of the pulpit" is spurious. Tragically, one of the results of "guaranteed appointments" for our clergy has been the protection of incompetent pastors. To avoid such misinterpretation, the *Discipline* should make clear that if, after a reasonable period of time and sincere efforts to match the talents of the pastor with the mission of a congregation, no congregation is found, then the connection has no further responsibility for the pastor. Humane means can be found for pastors to exit the annual conference, and means must be found to eliminate inept clergy. Our appointment system, dominated as it is by the clergy, will only work if the laypeople are confident that appointments will be made conscientiously. Without that confidence and trust, our system is destroyed.

We advocate, by disciplinary change, a method of appointments already in place in a number of conferences (Mississippi and New York, for instance), as well as in a majority of our larger churches. Basically, the plan allows local congregations to interview candidates prior to final appointment by the bishop. We absolutely affirm our constitution that places the ultimate power of appointment making in the hand of the bishop. Yet, prior to that appointment, the district superintendent shall propose potential pastors as selected by the bishop and cabinet. A pastor-parish relations committee shall be given a reasonable amount of time to submit additional names to the cabinet for interview. The pastor-parish relations committee must interview the potential pastors named by the bishop, and may interview any of its own suggested candidates, provided that the bishop gives approval. After this process, the pastor-parish relations committee and the pastors shall express their preferences. The bishop, however, shall not be obligated to follow the wishes of the committee or the pastors.

¶ 533: *Process of Appointment-Making.*—The process used in appointment-making shall include:

1. A change in appointment may be initiated by a pastor, a Committee on Pastor-Parish Relations, a district superintendent, or a bishop.

2. The bishop and the Cabinet shall consider all requests for change of appointment in light of the profile developed for each charge and the gifts and evidence of God's grace, professional experience, and family needs of the pastor.

3. When a change in appointment has been determined, the district superintendent should meet together or separately with the pastor and the Committee on Pastor-Parish Relations where the pastor is serving, for the purpose of sharing the basis for the

change and the process used in making the new appointment.

4. All appointments shall receive consideration by the bishop and the district superintendent(s) and the Cabinet as a whole until a tentative decision is made.

5. The **consultation** process used in making the new appointment shall include **the following**:

a) **The district superintendent shall provide to the receiving Committee on Pastor-Parish Relations the name(s) of potential pastor(s) as selected by the bishop and Cabinet. The committee may submit additional name(s) to the district superintendent and bishop.**

b) **Pastors contemplating a move may, through their district superintendent, request that their names be included on the lists of names being submitted to a particular church or churches.**

c) **The committee shall meet with any potential pastor(s) named by the bishop and may meet with any of its own suggested candidates, provided the bishop gives approval.**

d) **After the meetings, the committee and the potential pastor(s) shall express their preferences to the district superintendent and bishop. Following the gathering of this information, the bishop and cabinet shall make the projected appointment. The bishop shall not be obligated to follow the wishes of the committee or of the potential pastor(s) (¶ 531).**

e) **When the bishop names the projected appointee for the church/charge, the appointee, Committee on Pastor-Parish Relations, and district superintendent shall consult together on**

issues of ministerial and congregational expectations. The district superintendent shall maintain a permanent record of these expectations.

~~6. The district superintendent shall confer with the receiving Committee on Pastor-Parish Relations about pastoral leadership (¶ 532.1).~~

~~7. When appointments are being made to less than full-time ministry, the district superintendent shall consult with the ordained minister to be appointed and the Committee on Pastor-Parish Relations regarding proportional time, salary, and pension credit and benefit coverage.~~

We know the major objections to such consultation. Some say it will be too much work for the bishop and district superintendents. Yet, is not pastoral appointment their major ministry within our connection? Others say congregations do not know what sort of pastor they need. We trust congregations to work with the district superintendents and bishops more than we trust cabinets working alone. Still others fear superficial judgments based upon age, ethnicity, and gender (as if such superficial judgments are not now being made by cabinets!). We believe that God-given talent will overwhelm our biases. Good pastors will always be in demand. We have heard concern that some pastors will not interview well and are unskilled at presenting themselves. What do they do every Sunday in the pulpit? Overall, our proposed system is based upon openness, choice, dialogue, and attention to the needs of congregations and gifts of clergy. It is long overdue.

Gone are the days when congregations will simply take whomever the conference chooses to send. Even as we write this, we hear of a conference in which 20 percent of the churches seeking a new pastor will cut the salary. Is this a sign that congregations have less to spend, or is it a sign that they no longer trust the system? Consultation must be real, not just existing on paper. While we believe that this system will greatly improve clergy morale, our main justification for this change in pastoral appointment-making is based on our desire to strengthen and undergird the mission of the local church. The great genius of Wesleyan organization was that "form follows function." Structure must be based upon the mission of the church, not the other way around.

In all our debates about which structures and procedures best serve us, our judgment must favor that which best serves the mission of the local congregation. We trust local congregations. We believe local congregations must define their own mission, choose their own administrative and programmatic structure, have the right to revise their apportionments, participate in the appointment of their pastors, and be held accountable for the costs of their pastoral leadership. It is time to trust that local congregations, led by faithful laity and clergy, can make responsible decisions and be held responsible for ministry. Healthy congregations will lead to a healthy connection.

Praise the Lord!
A laywoman who participated in our discussion of
"Empower the Local Church"

Chapter 3

REFORM THE ANNUAL CONFERENCE

EVERY SEAT IN THE AUDITORIUM was taken. People sat outside on chairs. It was the closing session of annual conference, a grand service of worship, a service that included the reading of the pastoral appointments. The bishop preached well. The singing was enthusiastic. With an awesome sense of responsibility, the bishop asked that all clergy stand and hear their appointments. At the end, two laypersons were overheard to say, "*This* is what annual conference is all about. I just wish we hadn't wasted the preceding three days."

We acknowledge a great yearning among our people to restore our "historic Wesleyan connectionalism." The difficulty is that the system we now have is so far removed from the system of Wesley, Asbury, Boehm, and Otterbein, that we would not know historic connectionalism if we saw it.

The Wesleyan movement began as a yearly gathering of John Wesley's "traveling preachers," who met to worship, to report on their work during the past year, and to receive their assignments for the year ahead. The historic and still primary function of the annual conference is the recruitment, training, and assignment of clergy. All else is secondary.

Anyone familiar with the annual conference today will see how far we have diverged from its originating purpose. The once lean, missionally focused annual conference came to resemble the shape of American business of the 1950s or the federal government of the 1960s—large, complex, unwieldy, rule driven, preoccupied with procedure, expensive to operate, difficult to change, and tough to motivate.

A 1994 General Council on Ministries survey of the delegates to all annual conferences found that 71 percent of all lay delegates believed that "the *Discipline* should be revised to permit each annual conference to organize its work in its own way."

Today, annual conferences act as if they are *the* church and the local congregations are branch offices or franchises for the annual conference. Decisions flow from the top down, from the annual conference to the local church. Annual conference delegates, clergy and lay, vote on apportionments, start new programs, and are then expected to return to their local congregations and report on what the annual conference expects of them in the coming year. As Bishop Bruce Blake has said, "Program and resourcing of local congregations has shifted from the district to the conference level. This has been a source of confusion for thirty years and has not been effective."

This arrangement encourages a paternalistic attitude in which annual conferences act toward local churches like parents of little children, deciding for the children what the parent thinks best. Much of this attitude is due to the clergy's domination of the annual conference. Too many annual conference clergy leaders are pastors frustrated with their local congregations, and they impose upon the annual conference their pet agendas.

The *Discipline* gives the impression that we have achieved democratic representation in our annual conferences, in which laity have an equal vote with the clergy on most matters. In reality, the clergy are far more dominant.

First, few lay delegates are willing to take vacation from their jobs for the business conducted by most annual conferences. Many votes are taken with only a portion of the lay delegates in attendance. Few annual conferences have been willing to meet on weekends, which would be more convenient for lay participation, because weekend meetings of the conference are alleged to inconvenience the clergy.

Second, many of our lay leaders have been so successfully enculturated into the present system that, when they vote, they tend to vote more like the clergy than the clergy themselves. To the uninitiated layperson, our structure appears to be almost intentionally complicated, difficult to understand, and impossible to affect. A layperson who through years of meetings has finally learned how to work our complicated decision-making process well enough to change it is often a layperson who now sees little amiss in the process.

Some people have naively urged the laity to get mad, to get involved, and to change the system. But laypersons find that our system is heavily dominated by the clergy who manage the system for their professional benefit. The sheer complexity of the decision-making process, the heavy use of committees—large, unwieldy committees—render it a difficult process to change. Ironically, in the effort to make our church more democratic, to involve more people in the decision-making process, we have rendered our church unmanageable, the victim of manipulation by the few who understand and who profit from the present unwieldy structure.

Will has preached at dozens of annual conferences in the last decade. Without exception, the assembled conferences give the impression of an aging, predominantly Anglo gathering. The whole tone of the conference, the very way in which business is conducted, is the way Anglo, white-collar, corporate America does business (or, to be fair, once did business), with endless rules, committee reports, and parliamentary wrangling at a plodding tempo. The very notion of "business" in the annual conference is just that, only busy-ness. Committee reports, printed in the preconference journal, are read to the assembled delegates. Annual conference committees and agencies, eager to obtain more funding from the conference, give glowing reports to the conference. The rules, procedures, and reports express our lack of trust. Long, unproductive and superficial debates on various motions are common. Votes are usually decided by the will of the assembled clergy. Most of the delegates appear to be even older than the average United Methodist, because retired or semiretired persons can best afford the time required to be an annual conference delegate. Many of our most energetic and talented (and troublesome!) lay leaders, having seen the vast amounts of time wasted at annual conference, leave exhausted, depressed, and less enthusiastic (literally less filled with the Spirit) than when they came, and they refuse to be delegates again.

Because we must recover the primacy of the mission of the local church, the annual conference must recover a vision of itself as existing to support and encourage the mission of the local congregation. Each annual conference must ask itself, "What real business is needed from this assembly in a church which has suffered dramatic decline?" Tedious reporting from standing committees of the annual conference may be less important for us in the present moment than prayer and praise.

Rather than merely report on what we have done during another year of decline, perhaps we ought to spend time being led by our bishop in prayer that God grant us the courage to think boldly and to move courageously! Rather than merely gather more statistics on our sad state of decline, perhaps we ought to gather and tell stories about successful congregations where, despite the decline of our denomination at large, the Holy Spirit is moving at the local level.

We do have congregations that are demonstrating enthusiasm, excitement, and positive results. Interestingly, in a declining organization stories of success tend to be suppressed (remember the case of the "Churches of Excellence" in chapter 1) because the leadership has a stake in the rank and file believing that nothing can be done to stem the tide of decline, that the only story to be told is the story of failure. Where are those congregations where funds are being given by the laity for mission? Let them tell their stories; let the rest of our congregations mark well the reasons for their success in mission. Where are those local churches where people have moved beyond the safe confines of internal maintenance into bold new areas of service and witness? Let those stories be told; let the rest of us return home from annual conference newly invigorated and encouraged by the realization that God is still moving among the people.

The annual conference is best conceived as an annual assembly of clergy and lay delegates who worship and build consensus through prayer, praise, and story, rather than by voting and parliamentary procedure. At the end of the conference, in this scenario, clergy are appointed on the basis of the bishop and cabinet's assessment, in consultation with the congregation's missional requirements.

Annual conferences should eliminate all structures, staff, and budgets that are not directly supportive of congregationally based programs. The only programs that deserve support are those that the connected congregations voluntarily fund. The church best acts through persuasion rather than coercion, even if that coercion is based on some allegedly democratic vote from those at the top. If the gathered annual conference cannot find the means to encourage congregations to support a given program, then it should not short-circuit the need for persuasion and conversion by resorting to various apportionments and requirements by the annual conference.

Focus on Recruitment and Training of Clergy

By paring away all the conference-run, conference-directed programs, the annual conference can focus again upon the desperate need for quality clerical leadership for our congregations. With recruitment, training, and assignment of clergy as the primary tasks of the annual conference, conference boards of ordained and diaconal ministry can take even more seriously their crucial role in recruiting, training, and evaluating persons for ministry in local congregations.

The annual conference must be more aggressive in recruiting talented people for future clergy leadership. Conference youth events should accentuate pastoral ministry as a demanding, exciting vocation. Generally speaking, training that aims to produce more effective clergy leaders is more efficient than conference training events for the laity. Rather than spending so much time at short-term training events for lay leaders *outside* the local congregation, the conference ought to focus its energies on equipping the laity *within* the local congregation.

For several years, a staff member of the General Board of Discipleship tried to determine whether any short-term (less than two weeks) educational event for either clergy or laity made any long-term difference in the practices of the participants when they went back to their local church. This staff person could find no quantitative or qualitative difference which could be ascribed to participation in the training events. Lay leaders must be trained within their own congregations if there is to be substantive change. Teaching congregations (congregations whose staff and laity provide intentional training opportunities for others serving in similar congregations) are the most effective educational strategy for the laity.

Our Ministerial Education Fund (MEF) must be fundamentally reconfigured in order to enhance our church's training of clergy. While we have not offered specific proposals in our disciplinary recommendations, we believe that concerns regarding the MEF must be addressed by our general church. Overall, the MEF must be altered so that seminaries and seminarians are in significantly closer relationship with annual conferences and local congregations. The goal is that seminaries, seminarians, annual conferences, and congregations become more accountable to one another in the training of persons for parish ministry.

Today the Ministerial Education Fund raises approximately $15 million each year. This money is raised through a single line item apportionment to each local congregation. Of this money, 25 percent stays in the annual conference from which the money comes, and is used by conference boards of diaconal ministry and ordained ministry for continuing education of active ministers, grants and scholarships for clergy and diaconal ministers in training, and other areas of ministerial training. We believe that almost all of this money directed by annual conferences is well spent.

What happens next with MEF funds is our concern. According to the General Board of Higher Education and Ministry (GBHEM), of the total raised, 75 percent ($11.25 million) goes to GBHEM in Nashville, to be administered by this general board, primarily by its two divisions: Diaconal Ministry and Ordained Ministry. Of this $11.25 million, 84 percent ($9.45 million) then goes (via a formula created by the seminaries and general board members and staff) to our thirteen historic United Methodist seminaries. Most of the

money going to the seminaries is used for scholarship support for United Methodist seminaries. This system has
helped to create financially strong denominational seminaries
and has allowed many seminarians who attend United
Methodist schools to complete their work without significant
financial distress. The church has been generous because the
people in the local church really do want the best leaders they
can get.

But what about the other 16 percent ($1.8 million) that
Nashville retains? That money is used by GBHEM for
administrative costs (in the Division of Ordained Ministry:
$400,000, on top of the $385,000 World Service apportionment, most of which is used for salaries and benefits of
the staff), general church programs related to professional
ministry concerns, and general church scholarships such as
the Dempster scholarships for persons working on Ph.D.'s
who might one day teach at United Methodist schools.
Overall, MEF funds are used to support four groups:
United Methodist seminarians; United Methodist seminaries; the administrative and program costs of GBHEM; and
graduate level students. But is this the most efficient system to aid ministerial education?

Several concerns arise because of this system; primarily,
why should 75 percent of the money be funneled through
Nashville? The GBHEM, although staffed by skillful
people and guided by well-meaning voting directors, has
become the standard-bearer of the status quo. Although it
raises no money for MEF directly and primarily redirects
the money given by local congregations, the GBHEM
sets the criteria to guide these schools. The seminaries
are directly dependent upon Nashville, not upon the local
churches that gave the money. Should it be the GBHEM
to whom the seminaries must answer? Where is the
accountability between the United Methodist seminaries
and United Methodist congregations? It is time for the

seminaries to be in a direct relationship with the annual conferences and local congregations that give the money. When you forget who pays the bills, it is easy to forget whom you are serving.

While many other issues might also be addressed regarding the Ministerial Education Fund (the funding of United Methodist seminarians who do not attend a United Methodist seminary, for example), none is as important as why $1.8 million should go to Nashville. Today the General Board of Higher Education and Ministry stands between our seminaries and our congregations. In an age when we need more and better trained clergy, let us establish more dialogue and direct financial relationships between the seminaries and the annual conferences. Only in this way will we work together to prepare clergy for leadership in a new connection.

Delete the Conference Council on Ministries

¶ 726: Delete this paragraph (has to do with Conference Council on Ministries).

¶ 727: Delete this paragraph (has to do with conference Advance program).

¶ 728: Delete this paragraph (has to do with conference Board of Church and Society).

¶ 729: Delete this paragraph (has to do with conference Board of Discipleship).

¶ 730: Delete this paragraph (has to do with conference Board of the Laity).

¶ 731: Delete this paragraph (has to do with conference Board of Global Ministries).

¶ 732: Delete this paragraph (has to do with conference Board of Higher Education and Campus Ministry).

One way to reform our annual conferences is to eliminate the Conference Council on Ministries. The Conference Council on Ministries has become an impediment to the conferences focusing on the ministry of the local congregations. Created in 1968 as a coordinating effort (taken from the EUB system), the Conference Council on Ministries has become a self-perpetuating center of power. Conference staff are hired to fulfill Conference Council on Ministries objectives, rather than objectives that arise from the local congregations. Conference programs are created to prove that every conference agency is essential. The *Discipline* requires that every conference create parallel agencies to the general agencies. But for many clergy and laity, such conference activities do not serve the interests of the local church. Increasingly, busy and competent clergy and laity refuse to participate in conference programs, even though most of the space in conference newspapers is given over to articles written by and about Conference Council on Ministries staff touting programs which are mostly planned and directed by that staff. By attempting to serve everyone, the conference programs effectively serve no one. Local churches demonstrate, by their absence at such programs, that they have little interest in programs that are handed down from someone at the top. Huge amounts of money (much of it for salaries, travel, and lodging for meetings rather than for mission) are being wasted, along with a great amount of energy and time in the laborious but notoriously unproductive Conference Council on Ministries.

> If the Martians were to come and kidnap the whole Conference staff, it would be six months before anyone would know they were gone—and then, only by rumor.
>
> *Eugene Peacock, pastor*

Eliminating the Conference Council on Ministries would be rather simple. By deleting only a few paragraphs in the *Discipline*, the entire mandatory structure would be struck down. The Conference's Board of Ordained Ministry, Board of Diaconal Ministry, Committee on Episcopacy, Board of Pensions, Board of Finance and Administration, United Methodist Women, United Methodist Men, and other connectional structures would remain untouched, but areas devoted primarily to the agendas set by general program agencies and commissions would be deleted. On the positive side, each annual conference would be allowed to create the structure and the responsibilities it believes necessary for its own ministry.

Some innovative conferences are slowly devising a model better than that of the outmoded Council on Ministries. Conference programs and agencies are eliminated and conference staff now serve as local church consultants, on call to help undergird the programs of the congregations. An even better option would be for such consultants to contract with and to be paid by the congregations to whom they offer their services, as is the case with the Vision 2000 consultants. A consultant invited and employed by the congregation is taken more seriously than a free consultant.

What kind of ministries could survive so radical a change? Few of the currently mandated ministries may survive, but many others, such as Carolina Cross Connection and Ram's Rack, will thrive. Carolina Cross Connection (based on the nationally acclaimed Mountain Top program of Tennessee) began in a Lincolnton, North Carolina, United Methodist congregation. Begun by lay volunteers a few years ago, with help from a local church budget, Carolina Cross enlisted youth to spend one week repairing the homes of indigent members of the community. The program now runs youth mission teams out of four camps throughout the summer. In 1995, approximately one thousand youth worked for a week and shared their faith.

Ram's Rack is a ministry begun by the 350 member, 7 church cooperative United Methodist parish in Avery County, North Carolina. Begun in 1983 as a clothes closet and emergency fund, today it has 3 staff and a $100,000 budget. Each year it feeds, clothes, and furnishes the homes of people in an impoverished mountain region. It receives no conference support. These are only two programs. In a renewed connection, there will be more.

Reform the District Superintendency

We find ourselves sympathetic with much of our colleague Dolores Queen's dream for the district superintendency. After serving as a district superintendent, Queen knew that something was wrong with the way this office is presently configured. Disturbed that the role of district superintendent had become that of a perpetual fund-raiser for the conference, she formulated a proposal that included (1) eliminating the position of district superintendent as it is currently configured, (2) eliminating charge conferences and assigning leadership to "competent elders" in each district, and (3) decentralizing conference programming responsibilities by replacing district superintendents with "carefully chosen and thoroughly equipped 'proactive' district resource persons whose responsibility would be to serve as a consultant/resource person for local congregations."

Despite our sympathy with much of this plan, we recognize that some sort of district superintendency will survive. Therefore, while the office of district superintendent may be retained, it must be reformed. Transformation of the church's structure will be most painful for those district superintendents whose primary task has become the raising of money for and the care and feeding of the old connection.

> ¶ 521: Insert a new §6—6. **Travel outside the district shall not exceed 20% of the total work of the district superintendent.**

The main function of the district superintendent today is raising denominational funds by urging the payment of assigned apportionments. Too often, the fund-raising responsibilities of the district superintendent have placed superintendents in an adversarial role with both fellow clergy and the congregations under their care. An increasing amount of the district superintendent's time is being spent on fund-raising, administering the conference, and going to Conference Council on Ministries meetings. This direction must be reversed, as it is detrimental to the life of the local congregation.

After being sent to an aging, inner-city congregation, I saw the need for us to rethink our mission. We had lost half of our membership and half of our budget in the past twenty years. Something had to be done. So I led the congregation through a painful process of evaluation. Out of that process came the rather amazing decision to move the church to a different location.

Three years of self-sacrificial giving later, we were in our new building, with a growing, vibrant congregation. That very year, our district superintendent came to our charge conference and, after listening to our reports on our progress, stood up and lambasted us for not accepting our full share of the conference apportionments.

I was furious. Not only was that a cruel thing to do to our people during their current effort, but it was also stupid. In a year or so this congregation will be giving much more to the annual conference than would ever be possible in our earlier decline. . . . At least it would be giving much more if the district superintendent had not scolded us.

A pastor in South Carolina

———————

To enable district superintendents to spend more time with local churches, we should also eliminate the District Council on Ministries. This change retains a District Committee on Ordained Ministry, Committee on District Superintendency, and United Methodist Women, Men, and Youth. Such cuts eliminate ten pages from the *Discipline*, yet still allow each district to determine its own needs and structure. If there is one thing worse than a District Council on Ministries that does nothing, it is one that tries to do something! Meeting a couple of times a year, with an elaborate structure, trying to dream up a rationale for meeting, the District Council on Ministries is our present system at its nonsensical worst. Recently, one district sent a survey form to every pastor, lay leader, and administrative board or council chair in the district asking what the District Council on Ministries should do. After two months, not one single response had been received. The District Council on Ministries then had a one-day retreat to discuss why no one responded!

The growth of consultation between cabinets, bishops, congregations, and clergy is a good thing. Yet too often, "consultation" becomes yet another example of the cleri-

¶¶ **753-755:** Delete these paragraphs (have to do with district director of Church and Society, district director of Ethnic Local Church Concerns, and district director of Religion and Race).

¶ **757:** Delete this paragraph (has to do with district Board of the Laity).

¶ **762.3:** The functions of the district Council on Youth Ministries . . . ~~d) to cooperate with the programming and ministry of the district Council on Ministries as it serves to provide leadership training to persons in the district.~~

calization of our connection, where the career desires of pastors take precedence over the mission of the congregations. In a recent survey in the Western North Carolina Conference, clergy were "consulted" by their cabinet more than twice as often as local pastor-staff relations chairs were. In response, one astonished district superintendent said, "Local congregations usually don't really know what they need. But we do."

So the district superintendent told me that he had chosen our new senior pastor. He was a close friend of the district superintendent and "just what our congregation needed."

I found this interesting. Our district superintendent has not once worshiped in our church and hasn't yet met with our pastor-parish relations committee.

An associate pastor

We live in a new world in which old top-down authority patterns have been discredited. Fewer laity will accept the notion that "the cabinet knows best" with docile acquiescence. In the present crisis, we must take decisive steps enabling the laity to regain confidence in the administration of our appointment system. The best way for them to regain that confidence is by active participation in the system.

We believe that consideration should be given to resurrecting the work of the Presiding Elder as a model for our district superintendents. Until the 1930s, the Presiding Elder's role was to visit and to lead worship in every congregation in the district four times a year, and to recruit and mentor new pastors in the church.

Empower the Bishop in the Annual Conference

Related to a revisioning of the district superintendent's role is a reconsideration of the activities of our bishops. As they preside at annual conference, our bishops often seem like passive parliamentarians. The cabinet makes its report, but rarely does the bishop make a sustained statement of what she or he envisions. We recommend eliminating reports by cabinets to annual conferences and replacing them with a report by the bishop.

Some of our cabinets have assumed more authority in the appointment making process because our bishops are so often absent from their annual conferences. The *resident* bishop in each area must assume again her or his primary role of setting appointments. Because bishops are the chief personnel officers for the church, we desperately need them to make informed, knowledgeable, bold, and prayerful pastoral appointments. It is reasonable to expect about 80 percent of the bishop's time to be spent within the bounds of the annual conference.

> ¶ 514.3: To travel through the connection at large
> .... Such travel outside the Annual Conference(s)
> to which the bishop is assigned shall not exceed
> 20% of the total work of any resident bishop.

Some people argue that we cannot expect our bishops both to be more involved in annual conferences and to assume more responsibility for the general church. We disagree. The bishop's primary responsibility must be to the annual conference. But with more power in the general church (rather than following the will of agencies), bishops will be able to prioritize their time. Likewise, our proposals will cut many time-consuming responsibilities, such as approving every national meeting of every group (a current responsibility of the General Council on Ministries). We believe bishops can supervise the general church in about nine weeks a year. As one bishop said to us, "Give us the power, and we'll save ourselves from wasting our time as we do now." The majority of bishops with whom we have spoken believe our recommendations are achievable.

If the local congregation is to regain prominence, the bishop must spend significant time there—not in the conference office, not in gatherings solely with clergy—time to see firsthand the work of the congregation and to undergird its ministry.

In recent decades bishops have been expending more time and energy in travel related to the general oversight of the connection. A Conference Council on Ministries director in Texas recently stated that his bishop was out of the conference 50 percent of the time during the past year. Our bishops simply must be focused upon pastors and congregations within their annual conference. Just as our pastors need to be evaluated on their performance not in the annual conference but in their assigned congregations, so our bishops need to be held accountable to their work among the congregations of the annual conference.

We yearn for annual conferences where the yearly meeting is spirit-filled and thriving congregations tell their stories . . . where significant attention will be given to recruiting and training clergy . . . where the elimination of the Conference Council on Ministries in the district and annual conferences will enable new, lean, and focused organizations to grow . . . where restructured roles for district superintendents will enable them to assist local congregations more effectively . . . and finally, where bishops will be more focused on appointing the right clergy to the right congregations. Then, we have every confidence that annual conferences will be strong and exciting.

Chapter 4

REFORM THE GENERAL CHURCH

OVER THE LAST TEN YEARS, there have been bishops in every jurisdiction who have taken on the system and strove for reform. We are aware of courageous leaders who, in different ways, have challenged the current system and tried to emphasize the needs of local congregations. We are also aware that each has created significant backlash from pastors who feared that the entrenched seniority system might be threatened, from laity who distrusted anyone in authority, and from their episcopal colleagues who felt personally challenged. Unless we make some specific changes in the way our church is structured, we fear such strong, creative leadership will be again beaten down and replaced by more traditional leadership who promise not to rock the ark.

In a church that is overmanaged and underled, we desperately need our bishops to become leaders in the decentralization and creation of a new connection. Our general agency structure must be radically altered. Our present denominational structure of competing and balancing powers—a weak Council of Bishops, a quadrennial General

Conference, remote and virtually independent general agencies, councils and commissions, and ideological special interest caucuses—results in no one speaking to or for the church. We have rendered our bishops isolated, limited managers of a dysfunctional system.

Persons in key positions in The United Methodist Church today are primarily managers and not leaders. *Leaders* are persons with a vision that they are able to articulate. They can name the needs, desires, and hopes of the people. They have a charisma that inspires confidence. . . . Leaders establish new institutions; they revitalize and reform old ones. . . . In contrast, *managers* accept the validity of the institutional *status quo* and give their attention to its maintenance. They see that everything is done correctly by the proper person and consistent with precedent. They write and revise policy manuals; the machinery is oiled and polished. . . . the institution becomes a means in itself, rather than a means to serve a larger goal. . . . It does not matter whether the manager thinks of himself or herself as a political "liberal" or "conservative"; any change is threatening and will be resisted. . . . The United Methodist Church is dominated by managers.

Rekindling the Flame, 58-59

After the 1970 General Conference, Bishop Nolan B. Harmon, a professor of Methodist studies at Candler School of Theology, announced to his polity class, "Forget everything I taught you about our church's structure. It has all been changed. And you will spend the rest of your careers cleaning up the mess General Conference just created."[1]

We must undo the misguided actions of the 1968 and 1972 General Conferences, restore the power of the episcopacy and the Council of Bishops, and again make general agencies accountable to local congregations.

Electing Bishops

Our present system of electing bishops has not served us well. Admittedly, there is a sense in which we got the managers we wanted. Managers are keepers of the status quo. They promise not to trouble the present order, reassuring us that the old thinking and the old rules will remain securely in place. They concern themselves with internal management rather than with needs and challenges (i.e., mission) external to the maintenance of the organization.[2] Those who have been elected by the old order, with the old thinking, are those who benefited from a politicized election system. These may not be the best persons to look to for change in the system.

The wonderful truth is that, as Christians, we are not left to our own devices. The Holy Spirit constantly intrudes among us, prodding us. In our better moments, we United Methodists know that, by the grace of God, we are called for more.

If we are to improve the present episcopal election system, we must rescind that portion of the *Discipline* which now permits the formal nomination of episcopal candidates.

¶ 506. Delete this paragraph (has to do with the process by which candidates for bishop are nominated).

That which was once permitted has become virtually the only means of election. One of the goals of this "favorite son or daughter" process was to pull episcopal election politics out of the "back room," forcing the process into the light of public scrutiny and debate. Unfortunately, the actual results of the new episcopal election process have tended to be the election of bishops who, having jumped through so many hoops, having had to appear acceptable to so many conflicting constituencies on their road to the episcopacy, having been ground down smooth in the arduous election process, have nothing left with which to lead the church. The current process shifts the election from a search for persons who are called to the difficult role of leader of the connection to a search for persons who are able to put together a coalition of various interest groups in order to be elected.

Added to this, the formation of caucuses that vote as blocs must be prohibited at jurisdictional conferences. Such a prohibition was proposed and adopted at the 1992 Southeastern Jurisdictional Conference, though it is uncertain how it shall be implemented. Caucuses nominating their own candidates, as well as an elaborate system of "vote swapping" at jurisdictional conference, has generally produced bishops who are guaranteed managers. Candidates on the cutting edge, controversial leaders (most good leaders have always been controversial to someone), agents of change are passed over in favor of the "good soldiers," those who have led relatively nonconflicted lives loyal to their home annual conference, the annual conference where they will never serve as bishop. Talented leaders refuse to consider the episcopacy, abhorring a time-consuming and ultimately degrading election process.

A notable exception to the present grinding and unproductive episcopal election process was the election in 1984 of Leontine Kelly in the Western Jurisdiction. She was elected as a member of the Virginia Conference. In 1988, Susan Morrison was elected in the Northeast Jurisdiction, although she was not the candidate of her conference. Both of these able women truly believe their election indicated the presence of the Holy Spirit. We must dismantle the present episcopal election process to give more room for the Holy Spirit to intrude among us!

Another, perhaps more radical possibility is to abolish altogether the jurisdictional conferences and again have our bishops elected at General Conference. The jurisdictional system was created, in great part, to enable the southern conferences to retain some of their local autonomy and power when the northern and southern Methodist churches were merged. We look back fondly to the day when E. Stanley Jones, one of the greatest twentieth-century missionaries, won election not while campaigning at General Conference, but while on the mission field. He then declined the election, stating that his ministry was to the world more than to the institution! The last time we elected truly national figures to the episcopacy was in 1944. Now is the time to move back to national elections.

Dennis Campbell of Duke Divinity School agrees that we should abolish jurisdictions and elect bishops at General Conference (or alternatively, have jurisdictional conferences meet only at the site and at the time of General Conference to elect bishops), eliminate official annual conference endorsements, and prohibit bloc voting. Campbell further argues that bishops should be assigned on the basis of missional need without regard to the regional origin of the bishop. He calls for a recovered sense of the theological meaning of superintendency, and the recognition that while the Council of Bishops has need of persons of diversity, the episcopal office is too important for a person to learn "on the job." [3]

Reform the Council of Bishops

The Council of Bishops must also be given more power to set the agenda of the total connection. Today, the bishops elect a president who assumes the one-year office in addition to every other responsibility of an effective bishop. The president is assisted by one part-time adminis-trative secretary along with the secretary of the Council of Bishops (who also assumes the position in addition to her or his responsibilities as an effective bishop). The president has little real power and primarily chairs meetings. The Council needs to elect a full-time president who will serve for an entire quadrennium, and who may speak for the church and give direction.

Insert a new paragraph after ¶ 57, to read: **There shall be a president of the Council of Bishops who shall be an effective bishop elected by the Council of Bishops for one quadrennium. The election shall take place one year prior to the quadrennial election of bishops. The president shall assume office on the date specified by the General Con-ference as the effective date of assignment for all bishops for the quadrennium. The president shall serve in this office full time to facilitate the work of the Council of Bishops.**

The historic role of bishops in the church is, by their leadership and visible presence, to ensure the unity of the church and its link with the apostolic faith. A church is connected, not by its rules and its apportionments, but rather by its bishops. Remember Francis Asbury. Yet today, we are a ship without a captain. Our episcopacy has been captured by inappropriate, bureaucratic notions of leadership, rendering our bishops into "CEO's," top-level bureaucrats who administer rules, when, biblically and his-torically, bishops are our chief pastors whose presence ensures the unity, catholicity, and apostolicity of the church. The primary historic role of bishops is to enable the church to worship and serve the Triune God, not to administer the church. Wesley knew the necessity of the office of bishop. The main means of protecting our church from fragmentation, congregationalism, and heresy is not our *Discipline* but rather our bishops.

¶ 527: Renumber §4 as §3 and renumber §3 as §4, revised and expanded as follows: **4.** In order to exercise meaningful leadership, the Council of Bishops is to meet at stated intervals. The Council of Bishops is charged with the oversight of the spiritual and temporal affairs of the whole Church, to be executed in regularized consultation and cooperation with other councils and service agencies of the Church; **in particular, the council shall facilitate the Church's program life as determined by the General Conference and encourage, coordinate, and support the general agencies as they serve on behalf of the denomination. In this role, it shall:**

a) Study missional needs and propose priorities of the general church, and, when necessary, adjust emphases between sessions of the General Conference.

b) Establish the processes and relationships pertaining to the coordination and funding of the ministries and program emphases of the denomination through its general agencies and minimize unnecessary overlapping or conflicting approaches to the local church and the Annual Conferences.

c) Enhance the effectiveness of our total ministries by reviewing and evaluating the performance of the general program agencies and their responsiveness to the needs of the local churches and Annual Conferences.

Between ¶ 527 and ¶ 528, insert a new paragraph
to read as follows:

¶ ____. *Specific Responsibilities.*—**The responsibilities of the Council of Bishops shall include, but
not be limited to, the following:**

**1. Upon a two-thirds vote of the members of the
council present and voting, to make changes in missional priorities or special programs necessitated by
emergencies or by other significant developments
between General Conferences which substantially
affect the life of the Church, and to make adjustments in budget allocations accordingly; provided
that such adjustments are made within the total
budget set by the previous General Conference; and
provided, further, that such adjustments are made
after consultation with the affected boards and
agencies and approval by a two-thirds vote of the
General Council on Finance and Administration.**

**2. To take the following actions, in sequence,
with respect to recommendations to the General
Council on Finance and Administration for the
allocation of general church program funds to
general program agencies:**

**a) The Council of Bishops shall, in consultation
with the General Council on Finance and Administration and the general program agencies,
develop recommendations to the General Council
on Finance and Administration on needs of the
general program agencies for the programs, missional priorities, and special programs.**

**b) The Council of Bishops shall receive the
recommendation the General Council on Finance
and Administration proposes to make to the Gen-**

eral Conference as to the total general program agency budgets.

c) The Council of Bishops, after reviewing both the program priorities and the total funds available to the general program agencies, shall recommend to the General Council on Finance and Administration the amount of the budgets of each of those agencies, within the total sum proposed by the General Council on Finance and Administration for distribution among such agencies.

d) Only when the Council of Bishops and the General Council on Finance and Administration agree on the allocations to several general agencies shall these budgets be recommended to the General Conference by the General Council on Finance and Administration.

e) Before the beginning of each year the General Council on Finance and Administration shall determine and communicate to the Council of Bishops the sum available at that time from general church program agency contingency funds to meet requests for additional funding from the general program agencies. The Council of Bishops shall be authorized to approve allocations to the general program agencies for such additional program funding up to the limit so established. No money shall be allocated by the Council of Bishops from this source for general administrative costs, fixed charges, or capital outlay without approval by the General Council on Finance and Administration.

f) The Council of Bishops shall receive from the General Council on Finance and Administration copies of the proposed annual budgets of the general program agencies, in order that it may review such budgets in relation to the program proposals made by those agencies in their quadrennial budget requests.

3. To designate, in cooperation with the General Council on Finance and Administration, the general agency to undertake a special study ordered by the General Conference when the conference fails to make such a designation.

4. To assign responsibilities for implementation of themes, missional priorities, and/or special programs initiated between sessions of the General Conference to the general program agencies or to special task forces created by the Council of Bishops.

5. To assure the development of a unified and coordinated program for promoting of the connectional ministries of the Church.

6. To recommend to the General Conference the number and timing of special days which are to be observed on a churchwide basis; provided that the General Council on Finance and Administration shall make recommendations to the General Conference as set forth in ¶ 906.11 regarding the special days to be observed with offering; and provided further, that the Council of Bishops and the General Council on Finance and Administration may authorize a special financial appeal in an emergency.

7. To resolve any overlapping in structure or functions or lack of cooperation among the general program agencies.

8. To study the connectional structures of The United Methodist Church and, after consultation with the general agencies, recommend to the

General Conference such legislative changes as may be appropriate to effect desirable modifications of existing connectional structures. Any such proposed legislative changes that would affect general fund budget allocations shall be studied in connection with the General Council on Finance and Administration and shall be recommended to the General Conference by these two councils acting in concert.

9. To review and evaluate the effectiveness of the general program agencies in fulfilling the ministries assigned to them (see ¶ 802.3).

10. The general secretary of each general program agency that is accountable to the Council of Bishops shall be elected annually by ballot of the Council of Bishops upon the nomination of the agency involved. Any general secretary of a general program agency who has not been elected by the Council of Bishops shall not serve in such capacity beyond the end of that calendar year. Each program agency shall elect annually by ballot its deputy and associate general secretary(ies) and may elect or appoint such other staff as may be necessary.

11. To report to the General Conference for its approval a summary of all decisions and recommendations made dealing with program changes and structure overlap.

12. To review, with the program agencies, all valid resolutions and positions adopted by the General Conference, and recommend to the General Conference the removal of time-dated materials.

13. **To receive reports from and refer matters to the General Commission on Christian Unity and Interreligious Concerns on the participation of The United Methodist Church in the various aspects of ecumenism.**

14. **To organize the Advance Committee which shall have general oversight of the Advance program.**

15. **To act in concert with the General Council on Finance and Administration to establish a procedure for making a quadrennial review, initiating proposals, and/or responding to proposals by the general agencies regarding the location of headquarters and staff and report the same to the General Conference. (See ¶ 907.2.)**

In order to fulfill their theological leadership function, bishops must be empowered to set the agenda of the denomination. One of the saddest sights of any General Conference is to see the Council of Bishops sit on a platform in front of the voting delegates along with the potted plants. They preside and handle parliamentary procedure, but have no control over either the agenda or the calendar. The bishops begin General Conference with an episcopal address, but it is not released in advance of General Conference.

¶ 12.1: The General Conference shall be composed of **the effective bishops of The United Methodist Church and** not less than 600 nor more than 1,000 **additional** delegates, one half of whom shall be . . . .

Everyone listens politely before moving on to the real agenda—thousands of petitions, the majority of which, printed in the advance *Daily Christian Advocate,* come from general agencies or special interest groups. Bishops should be given a vote at General Conference. Likewise, at annual conference, bishops should set the agenda and control the calendar.

Today, every person who has ever been elected to the episcopacy is invited by the Council of Bishops to its meetings. The Council of Bishops should be limited to active ("effective" is the way the *Discipline* puts it) bishops, rather than including all retired bishops. Its votes ought to be binding in every member of the Council, and its mutual oversight of its member bishops should be strong.

> ¶ **50:** There shall be a Council of Bishops composed of all the **effective** bishops of The United Methodist Church.

During a 1991 debate in the Council of Bishops regarding ordination and consecration services, two-thirds of all remarks came from retired bishops who reminisced about how it used to be. Although only active bishops may vote, it was difficult for the active bishops to know how one another felt before the vote. While there is value in experience, would a local congregation invite any person who previously served on the administrative board or council to sit on the front row at each meeting and to speak on any and every issue? Yet this is how the Council of Bishops often operates. A declining organization tends to focus on yesterday rather than tomorrow. We know a number of bishops who privately support excluding our retired bishops. They will be reluctant to support our position publicly. It is time for the church to support the active bishops.

¶ 510. *Status of Retired Bishops.*—A retired bishop is a bishop of the Church in every respect **except for membership in the Council of Bishops** ~~and continues to function as a member of the Council of Bishops in accordance with the Constitution and other provisions of the Discipline~~. **Upon retirement, the membership of a bishop shall revert to the Annual Conference of which the bishop was a member at the time of his or her election, or its successor.**

¶ 510.1: Retired bishops ~~may participate in the Council of Bishops and its committees but without vote. They~~ may preside over sessions of an Annual Conference, Provisional Annual Conference, or Mission if requested to do so . . . . However, when a retired bishop is appointed by the Council of Bishops to a vacant episcopal area or parts of an area under the provisions of ¶ 510.3 or ¶ 511.2, that bishop may function as a bishop in the effective relationship, **including membership in the Council of Bishops**.

Now there is something to be said for allowing our older bishops to participate in the deliberations of the Council of Bishops, because only our older bishops remember a church which was growing rather than declining! We currently have bishops who have never served a growing congregation. Our older bishops could remind us that our present structure is a relatively recent creation, a product of a particular period in our recent history, a human creation which can be humanly changed. Yet, their presence at COB meetings costs us approximately $100,000 a year.

Of even greater concern, according to a 1995 survey by the General Council on Ministries, though persons fifty and over constitute only about 26 percent of the American population, they constitute about 61 percent of The

United Methodist Church. By the year 2000, if present trends continue, two-thirds of all United Methodists will be over fifty years of age. In a connection which has lost large numbers of its younger members, a denomination which is "graying" faster than the national population at large, and a connection in great need of major change, some of our older, more experienced members must defer to our younger leadership in order that our church might be more in touch with the spiritual needs of our younger constituency.

The Council must also offer greater supervisory oversight of its own membership. If there is little real supervision and oversight of individual United Methodist clergy, our impression is that there is virtually no collegial supervision of our bishops. When one bishop was rendered almost incompetent by a stroke, two years passed before an informal group of bishops had the courage to convince this bishop to take early retirement. No matter what the Council of Bishops votes, each bishop is free to follow her or his own desires. The only means of accountability—and a poor means of ensuring collegial leadership—is for someone to take a bishop and the bishop's decisions to the Judicial Council.

In 1968, General Conference felt that our church could best be led by taking power away from our bishops and giving it to a vast and growing bureaucracy (principally the General Council on Ministries). In the last two decades our church has demonstrated the fallacy of this bureaucratic mentality. Our agencies have become self-protective, self-perpetuating bureaucracies which spend much of their time between General Conferences preparing new legislation for the next General Conference, in order to expand and to protect themselves.

This power should be returned to the Council of Bishops. Likewise, by simple disciplinary changes, let the

Council of Bishops evaluate the general agencies, coordinate the general agencies, and most significantly, elect general secretaries (the head administrators) of the general agencies.

Change the General Agencies

To a greater or lesser degree, each of our general agencies has served our church to the best of its ability within the present structure. Competent persons who clearly love our church have led these agencies. Among the essential functions our general agencies, boards, and commissions have performed for us are the following:

— The General Board of Church and Society reminds our church of our Christian witness in an increasingly secular culture.
— The General Board of Discipleship serves local churches with programs and resources in education, evangelism, stewardship, lay ministries, and worship.
— The General Board of Global Ministries supports over 600 overseas missionaries and the United Methodist Committee on Relief.
— The General Board of Higher Education and Ministry keeps our standards for schools high and supports many students through scholarships and programs of Christian discipleship on campus.
— The General Commission on Christian Unity and Interreligious Concerns unites us with the Body of Christ worldwide.
— The General Commission on Religion and Race reminds us of the sin of our racism and encourages redemptive acts of racial inclusiveness.
— The General Commission on the Status and Role of Women underscores the role of women in our

church and encourages the church to enable women to reach their full potential.

— United Methodist Communications produces superb print, video, and audio resources for the church and promotes the World Service Fund, the Advance, and other general church funds.

— The General Commission on Archives and History records and saves our historical documents.

— The General Board of Publication, The United Methodist Publishing House, provides services and resources for the church and the Christian community.

— The United Methodist National Youth Ministry Organization provides national gatherings and support for our future church leaders.

— Our general administrative agencies, the General Board of Pension and Health Benefits and the General Council on Finance and Administration, operate in a complex financial world with skill and prudence.

We have been blessed. But we can no longer allow these agencies to operate as functionally autonomous units. Many who labor within them experience great frustration with the present structure. In the 1994 General Council on Ministries survey, 66 percent of the annual conference delegates voted to reform our general agencies. Decreasing funds will require a restructuring of these agencies, councils, and commissions. We believe such restructuring ought to proceed from a careful consideration of the church's mission rather than from slashes and cuts in recurring financial crises, or even worse, slowly starving all of them by declaring a freeze on all funds.

Having increased the power of the episcopacy, there are at least two possible models for realigning the power of our bureaucracy, providing for a decentralized and simplified structure. The model we propose is for the Council of Bishops simply to replace the General Council on Ministries and

¶¶ **1001-1007:** Delete these seven paragraphs (have to do with General Council on Ministries).

assume the role of coordination. Then allow the remaining general agencies, councils, and commissions to prove themselves to local congregations. Because local churches can revise their apportionments, agencies that support the ministry of local congregations will receive funding. Those that cannot justify their worth will cease to exist. Such a proposal will prod agencies to cut unnecessary programs, not on the basis of a particular ideology, but on the basis of the support of local congregations. To limit the agencies from spending too much money promoting themselves to the detriment of their ministry, we would limit the agencies to spending no more than 10 percent of their budget on self-promotion. To give them access to additional sources of income, we would allow them to approach individuals and foundations for support. In this model the program agencies such as the General Board of Discipleship and the General Board of Global Ministries could become self-funding resource centers that serve the local congregations.

¶ 912. *Support of the General Program Agencies of the Church.*—**Support of the general program agencies, commissions, and funds is basic in the financial program of The United Methodist Church. The Annual Conferences and local churches/ charges have the right to revise the apportionments for such agencies, commissions, and funds. Closely related to that right is the responsibility to support the general program agencies, commissions, and funds as one of the benevolent responsibilities of the church.**

> **1. The General Council on Finance and Adminis-tration shall recommend to each quadrennial session of the General Conference the amount of the quadrennial and annual apportioned budgets of each of the general program agencies, commissions, and funds and the method by which they shall be apportioned to the Annual Conferences. It shall be the responsibility of the council to facilitate sound fiscal and administrative policies and practices within and among the general agencies of the Church.**
>
> **2. No general program agency, commission, or fund shall spend over 10% (ten percent) of its budget to solicit apportioned funds or special gifts from individual donors or special groups, unless approval is first secured from the General Council on Finance and Administration.**

A second model, now being proposed by the General Council on Ministries, would leave the Council of Bishops as the locus for teaching and making appointments, but would then link all the current general agencies through a complex "interactive" web of groups and relationships. In this model, we hope that our episcopal leaders will have a primary voice in setting the course for connectional ministry, although the plan seems to upset the fruit basket while making no substantive changes that would produce new results. If the church adopts such a plan without also agreeing that agencies must be supported only through the voluntary gifts of local United Methodist congregations, it will simply reshuffle the deck without making any substantial changes in the bureaucracy.

A vivid depiction of the outdated, top-down, managerial

mentality prevalent in United Methodism is the importance given to the organizational form and work of the denominational agencies. There are 220 pages, or one-third of the text, of the current *Discipline* devoted to the organization and responsibilities of the general boards and agencies. Most are written by the agencies themselves to expand their influence. Thirty pages are devoted to local congregations.

Bishops chair many of our agencies, commissions, and councils. We give our bishops a front-row seat in which to observe the abuses and weaknesses of our agencies, but little power to change them for the better. The church should have much more faith in the leadership of the Council of Bishops than in assorted general agency leaders who lack the visibility, election, accountability, and historic theological justification of our bishops.

We would be light years ahead of where we are now if we simply abolished the General Council on Ministries and devoted that money and staff to the Council of Bishops.

A general agency chief administrator

One of the major difficulties in the general agency system is that, with the exceptions of the General Board of Pension and Health Benefits and the General Council on Finance and Administration, board members are chosen for the various agencies primarily on the basis of age, nationality, geographic region, gender, or race, and not also on the basis of their spiritual gifts, skills and knowledge. Some of our agencies are required to have at least one person from each annual conference. It is "recommended" that one-third be clergy; one-third be laymen; one-third be laywomen; and 30 percent be members of designated ethnic minorities. In the two agencies that deal with money, particularly money which belongs to the clergy, members are chosen on the basis of expertise in addition to representation. Why do standards of expertise, experience, and demonstrated competence not apply to matters like evangelism, worship, and education?

In addition, a large percentage of each agency is elected by the agency itself. On *The United Methodist Book of Worship* Committee, one-third of the members had never had even one course in worship. Persons within our connection who had spent a lifetime acquiring and developing liturgical skills could serve only as consultants because they failed to meet gender, age, geographic region, and race requirements.

Ironically, our rules for composition have not made our church more representative and responsive to the needs of our various constituencies. While we have over 950 elected board members, few of them "represent" the local church. Democracy is what we wanted but not what we got because representation by region, age, sex, race, and so on were considered more important than expertise, skill, or service to the local church. Skilled, paid staff members became virtually the only knowledgeable people on the boards and agencies; they could easily dictate the topics for discussion and the agenda of the board or commission. Our church must reconsider the rationale for qualifications for persons serving on its general agency boards.

¶ 805.2: *General Program Board Membership.—a) Basic Membership.—*Each jurisdiction shall elect one person from each of its Annual and Missionary Conferences to each program board. In the jurisdictional

~~nominating process for membership on those boards,~~
~~special attention shall be given to the inclusion of~~
~~clergywomen, youth, (¶ 264.2), young adults (¶~~
~~264.3), older adults (¶ 264.5), persons with handicap-~~
~~ping conditions, and persons from small membership~~
~~churches. In order to ensure adequate representation~~
~~of racial and ethnic persons (Asian Americans, Black~~
~~Americans, Hispanic Americans, Native Americans,~~
~~Pacific Islanders), it is recommended that at least 30~~
~~percent of a jurisdiction's membership on each gen-~~
~~eral program board be racial and ethnic persons. It is~~
~~further recommended that the jurisdiction member-~~
~~ship on each program board incorporate one-third~~
~~clergy, one-third laymen, and one-third laywomen~~
~~(except as provided in ¶¶ 1204.1, 1412.2. See also ¶¶~~
~~1412.6, 1507.). The episcopal members shall not be~~
~~counted in the computation of the clergy member-~~
~~ship.° *Provided*, however, that effective immediately,~~
~~when a new Annual Conference or conferences are~~
~~created by a Jurisdictional Conference and come into~~
~~being following the Jurisdictional Conference, each~~
~~such new Annual Conference or conferences shall be~~
~~authorized to elect one person directly to General~~
~~Council on Ministries and each general program~~
~~board on which no person from the new Annual Con-~~
~~ference already has been elected by the Jurisdictional~~
~~Conference under the provisions of this paragraph.°~~
**Twenty-eight members shall be elected by the
Jurisdictional Conferences on a ratio providing
for an equitable distribution among the various
jurisdictions, based on the laity and clergy membership thereof. The secretary of the General**

Conference shall calculate the ratios and determine the number of members of each board to be elected by each jurisdiction; provided, however, that no jurisdiction shall be represented by fewer than two members on each board. Primary consideration shall be given to persons with specific expertise in the program areas of the general program agencies. Membership on each board shall be equally divided, as far as practicable, between ordained ministers and lay persons. It is recommended that persons elected by each jurisdiction be inclusive of women and ethnic groups. No other criteria shall be used for general board membership.

b) Episcopal Membership.—The episcopal membership of not less than ~~five~~ **three** nor more than ~~ten~~ **six** members shall be nominated by the Council of Bishops and elected by the General Conference . . . .

c) Additional Membership.—(1) ~~United Methodist~~ *Members from Central Conferences.*—~~Additional members shall be elected by each general program board in order to bring into the board persons with special knowledge or background which will aid in the work of the agency, to consider differing theological perspectives, and to perfect the representation of racial and ethnic persons, youth (¶ 264.2), young adults (¶ 264.3), older adults (¶ 264.5), women and men, person with a handicapping condition, and persons from small membership churches, and distribution by geographic area. There shall be not less than five nor more than nine additional members of each general program board. It is recommended that such additional membership shall maintain the one-third~~

~~laymen, one-third laywomen, and one-third clergy balance.~~ ~~In addition, each~~ **Each** board shall elect ~~six~~ **three** persons from the Central Conferences, and one alternate for each who may attend if the elected member cannot attend. ~~In the election of the Central Conference members, it is recommended that two be clergy, two be laymen, and two be laywomen.~~

Specifically, we propose that we reduce the number of voting members of general agencies by almost half. We can eliminate every quota (although the Judicial Council has ruled quotas unconstitutional, they do exist at every level) and insist that skill and spiritual gifts for the specific task of the agency be the primary criteria for election. Representation will be based on the size of jurisdictions. Likewise, we propose to eliminate agencies' appointing their own people to the boards. Today, several caucus groups have more power on the general boards than any annual conference or even jurisdiction. A number of smaller commissions, including the General Commission on Archives and History, United Methodist Communications, the General Commission on Christian Unity and Interreligious Concerns, the General Commission on Religion and Race, and the General Commission on the Status and Role of Women, appoint over 20 percent of their own membership.

¶ **2204.1:** The basic membership [of the Commission on the Status and Role of Women] shall be nominated and elected by the Jurisdictional Conferences . . . . ~~Each~~ **The** jurisdiction shall elect ~~six~~

twenty persons for membership **on a ratio providing for an equitable distribution among the various jurisdictions, based on the memberships
thereof; provided that no jurisdiction shall be
represented by fewer than two members.** It is
recommended that **at least half of the ~~six~~ members elected by each jurisdiction ~~there~~ be
women** ~~two laywomen, two laymen, one clergy-
woman, and one clergyman. Of the persons elected
by each Jurisdictional Conference, at least one
should be from a racial and ethnic group and at
least one shall be under thirty-one years of age at
the time of election.~~

These internal appointees owe their positions to the
commission that appointed them, and because almost all
of these extra members were General Conference delegates, will fight at General Conference to maintain the
status quo. Such changes will save millions of dollars
over the next quadrennium. Likewise, by having smaller
boards of qualified persons, they will be better able to set
policies that reflect a decentralized church.

Whatever model is put into effect, the overriding concern of all general agencies of our church must be to support the mission of local congregations. Today, despite
denials, each agency primarily serves the national connection as a whole, or subgroups unrelated to local congregations. It is more important to appease one of our many
self-interest groups than any local congregation. By
becoming self-funding resource centers that serve the local
church, agencies remaining after decentralization will be
those that enable local congregations to do what they cannot do without the general agency assistance.

The Upper Room, colleges, and other institutions already function with minimal support from our connection. The United Methodist Publishing House functions well with no support funds from our connectional system. They can be our models. Such organizations provide only resources needed as shown, in the case of the publishing house and The Upper Room by their sales, in the case of our seminaries and colleges by their enrollments. In one of our conferences, the conference children's home has for years fought any attempt to make it a line item in the list of conference apportionments. This children's home was confident that it could raise more money by taking its message to local churches and there to receive voluntary gifts rather than by forcing churches to fund it through the apportionment system.

Decentralize Funding of the General Church

The heart of our proposed reform of the general boards, commissions, and councils is to make every agency dependent upon the voluntary funding by local congregations on line item apportionments. *We do not propose the elimination of any agency.* To make such proposals is also to fall prey to the idea that someone up there at the top knows best.

¶ 248.14: . . . what amounts have been apportioned to it for ~~World Service and Conference Benevolences~~ **general church and Annual Conference program agencies and causes** . . . the importance of ~~World Service and Conference Benevolences~~ these apportionments . . . . ~~The World Service Fund is basic in the financial program of The United Methodist~~

> ~~Church. World Service on apportionment represents~~
> ~~the minimum needs for the mission and ministry of~~
> ~~the Church.~~ Payment ~~in full~~ of these apportionments
> ~~by local churches~~ is **one of** the ~~first~~ benevolent
> ~~responsibility~~ responsibilities of the Church ~~(¶ 912)~~.
> **Each Charge Conference shall have the right to
> revise the apportionment for each general agency,
> council, commission, and fund requested by the
> General Conference, except the Episcopal Fund
> and the funds for conducting General Conference;
> each apportionment from the jurisdiction; each
> apportionment from the Annual Conference,
> except the District Superintendents' Fund, pen-
> sion and benefits funds for pre-1982 service, the
> Equitable Compensation Fund, and the costs of
> Annual Conference meeting; and each apportion-
> ment from the district.** The district superintendent
> or designated agent shall also notify . . . .

Rather, *let local congregations, by their dollars, tell the church which agencies will prosper or fail.* This is the heart of our plan for decentralization.

Ronald E. Vallet and Charles E. Zech have provided the best comparative study of the financial decline within mainline denominations in their book *The Mainline Church's Funding Crisis: Issues and Possibilities.* Their research and analysis substantiates the need for the type of financial decentralization we are proposing:

> In 1993, United Methodists placed $3.3 billion in their churches' offering plates. Of this amount, $130.2 billion went to the denomination's national and churchwide efforts. Yet this was still short of budget expectations. Clifford Droke, head of the General Council on Finance and

Administration, reported that giving to churchwide "apportioned" funds . . . continued a trend of the past several years
of not reaching budget expectations. . . . The World Service
fund, which pays for world wide mission and national agencies, received $48.4 million—85.7 percent of its apportioned
amount. . . . Declining membership and benevolence giving,
reductions in staff, . . . and a growing unwillingness to fund
an old system indicated that The United Methodist Church
was operating in a maintenance mode, at best.[4]

Practically, voluntary funding from the local churches
will guarantee that those program activities most related to
local congregations—basic Christian concerns like evangelism, worship, stewardship, and mission—will continue.
Congregations will always need specific worship resources,
through which sales a worship unit can survive. We believe
congregations will continue to want to be a part of global
ministries, but ministries in which they have a new sense of
themselves as partners rather than paymasters. The rest
will either wither away or move to some sort of voluntarily
related, but not mandated, organization. For years our
church has been served by agencies with special interests
and expertise, such as the Order of Saint Luke (worship
renewal), Good News (evangelical renewal), and the
Methodist Federation for Social Action (social concern),
that receive no mandated funding and have no mandated
existence but which have done good work among the connection. Those with special concerns for our church—particular ethnic concerns, ministries to persons with special
needs, for example—must see that these needs are best
addressed through the work of tangential, voluntary organizations related to the connection but not mandated and
funded through measures dictated by the *Discipline.*
In *The Mainline Church's Funding Crisis,* Zech says that
the relationship of local congregations to the general
church today is most similar to how large corporations set
up franchises. Corporations grant franchises the rights to

the trademark (in our case the cross and flame), provide management training (seminaries), exert some control to limit liability (trustees), require fees (apportionments), and share profit or loss (this is what we are missing). The fatal flaw is that, unlike many franchisers, our local congregations have almost no say in the financial decisions of the larger church. As Zech says, this results in "denominational agents [i.e., mission board officials] maximizing their own goals over those of the church members." Zech believes our current denominational system has little chance of survival without structural changes. As he says, "a new relationship [between local congregations and the general church] must be developed that better meets the mission criteria of transparency, efficiency, and accountability."[5]

Zech then makes three recommendations, based on the work of Loren Mead in *The Once and Future Church* (Washington, D.C.: Alban Institute, 1991). In general, we agree with Zech's moderate proposal (as opposed to doing nothing or abolishing the system). Zech says that we ought to "totally eliminate mission boards' [our general boards, councils, and commissions] guaranteed funding and require them to compete" with other suppliers. Increased competition will require that the ministries of the general agencies be "transparent" (easily understood), "efficient" (requiring minimal upkeep), and "accountable" (through frequent updates). Without transparency, efficiency, and accountability, we fear our total system will collapse.

Lest some fear that the work of our national church would come to a grinding halt, we offer *The United Methodist Hymnal* as a good example of supplying the local church with local church money. The United Methodist Publishing House, a self-funding agency, chose to fund fully the development of our new hymnal. In 1984 the General Conference said that there was no money (and possibly little need) for this new resource. But the leaders of the publishing house decided that there *was* a local church need and took the risk. Over a period of four years, The United Methodist Publishing House invested well over one million dollars to pay for staff, meetings, and other related expenses of the hymnal's development. When the hymnal was released, The United Methodist Publishing House more than recovered its investment as local churches reviewed, then purchased nearly five million copies. Those who argue that we will not have good resources unless we forcibly fund the general agencies should consider the case of *The United Methodist Hymnal.*

A contrasting example of bureaucratic waste is *Quarterly Review,* which is funded through large subsidies from The United Methodist Publishing House and the General Board of Higher Education and Ministry. *Quarterly Review* says that it is "A Journal of Theological Resources for Ministry." Unfortunately, it has shown itself to be a journal that few pastors want. The subscription lists of *Quarterly Review* have never drawn more than a tiny fraction of United Methodist clergy (total paid subscriptions are now about 1700 out of 39,000 clergy), probably because clergy have better, more interesting scholarly publication alternatives in journals like *Theology Today, Interpretation,* or *First Things.*

Quarterly Review (a journal in which both of us have published articles) is subsidized by over $50,000 a year, an average subsidy of about $30 per subscriber per year (who pays much less than that per year).

Why is *Quarterly Review* so dull? It doesn't need to be interesting since it draws its funds, not from those who actually read it, but rather from two agencies of the church who pay for the production of a publication which has no constituency other than the need of a couple of agencies to justify themselves.

An editor of an independent clergy journal with a circulation five times larger than that of Quarterly Review.

The General Conference should eliminate all funding for the publishing units of the general agencies. These publishing units, such as Discipleship Resources and the myriad of published resources produced by the General Board of Global Ministries, the General Board of Church and Society, the General Commission on the Status and Role of Women, and others, often serve the internal needs of these organizations for identity and recognition rather than the mission of the local churches. All of these publications cost the agencies more than they bring in. Publications such as *The Interpreter* (at an annual cost of over $300,000 per year) appear to be mainly of value as a way for various staff members to tell local congregations why the services of a given general board or agency are essential. It is our observation that this information is important to the staff members who write the articles, but relatively unimportant to the ministry of the local church. If so, why publish? If pastors and laity in the local congregations do not want the resources, why make costly publication expenditures?

Subsidized projects may prove worthy if they serve the needs of local churches. For example, *Circuit Rider* is financed by The United Methodist Publishing House and is widely viewed as helpful because it addresses topics of interest to pastors while also providing a link between UMPH and a key constituency. This demonstrates that a self-supporting agency can meet the needs of the connection without depending upon apportionments.

The Upper Room is also a model of how a self-financed agency ought to conduct itself. On the basis of the sales of devotional books, The Upper Room is able to move into many other areas of church publication and programs in spiritual formation. In a bold, yet criticized move, in the late 1980s The Upper Room cancelled the magazine *Christian Home*. It was cancelled not because the articles were poor or because of a lack of love for families, but because it was losing money every month. The leaders of The Upper Room decided that if it could not sell, it must not be needed. At the same time, The Upper Room created the phenomenally successful and creative magazine *Weavings* and financed and pioneered effective continuing education in spiritual formation, all of which had to be fully self-funding. It has produced a wide array of Bible study, devotional, and worship resources. We see no reason why The Upper Room cannot continue, if not grow stronger, in a decentralized church.

Because it must sell books, The United Methodist Publishing House keeps its ear to the ground, attentive to what United Methodists actually want to read. *The United Methodist Hymnal* is an example of good things that can happen when the laity and the local congregations, rather than the ideological concerns of professional bureaucrats, set the agenda. In the spring of 1986, the United Methodist Hymnal Revision Committee voted not to include "Onward, Christian Soldiers" and "The Battle Hymn of the Republic" in the new hymnal. The decision made perfect sense to people like us who question the theological and musical value of these popular hymns. Professional liturgists and hymnologists praised the decision to delete them. Yet, when the decision was announced, the publishing house was deluged with telephone calls. Over twelve thousand letters were sent to the committee. The committee had tampered with hymns which were deemed essential to many of our congregations. Within weeks the Hymnal Revision Committee, realizing how these hymns were loved by laity and pastors in local congregations, reversed its decision. While we believe that there were strong arguments for not retaining these hymns, we more strongly support the committee's recognition that this hymnal and its hymns belonged to the churches of the connection. Would that local congregations had vociferously asserted themselves more often!

Many of those who serve in and profit from the general agencies will vehemently disagree with our analysis. Each one of them believes (with vision statements to back them up) that they serve local congregations. In fact, we fully expect a rash of self-promotional literature will appear prior to our next General Conference, praising the value of each agency for the local congregation. However, we have yet to know a local congregation who could even name our thirteen agencies, fourteen special funds, missional priorities, and so forth, let alone know their functions. This promotional effort should be seen as positioning to protect turf at the next General Conference.

Conclusion

Will had a number of members in one of his congregations who worked for the Bell System ("Ma Bell"). These persons had been attracted to Bell partly because the company had a reputation for stability and for "looking after" its loyal employees. Two of the people even had parents who worked before them for the Bell System.

"If you keep your head down and do your job, the company will take care of you," was how one of them described life in the old telephone company.

Then, in the 1980s the Supreme Court struck down the telephone company's monopoly. Suddenly, the Bell System found itself having to compete with dozens of other communications services. The company discovered that leaders in the old company were ill-suited to the demands of increased competition, aggressive sales, rapid technological innovation. Now, a decade later, after changes which were undoubtedly painful for many in the Bell System, a reorganized AT&T and the "baby bells" greet the future with optimism.

We understand that many of our denomination's leaders are comfortable in the old world, a world in which our denomination enjoyed a central role in North American Protestant church life, a world in which a clergyperson could join our system, refuse ever to rock the ark, and count on a lifetime of institutional security.

The choice is ours. We can continue down that time-worn path, continue to do business as usual, continue to drag along behind us a distant bureaucracy and careful, management-minded leaders who write rules and follow them. That is a way which leads, alas, not to life but to death.

We are confident that our living God has called us forth for more.

Afterword

THE FUTURE OF OUR CONNECTION

WE BEGAN BY INVITING YOU to a conversation, a reasoning together about the future of our beloved church. We have been forthright, and we welcome your response. We have been critical, and we are open to criticism. We have expressed hope, and we believe in the future of United Methodism. Now we focus upon the central question. What *is* the future of The United Methodist Church? A major question raised by our proposals for reform is, What will hold us together as United Methodists? Can so loose a structure still be called a denomination?

> Do efforts to decentralize and take initiative at regional and local areas mean the end of Methodist connectionalism as we know it? As we know it, maybe. An end of Methodist connectionalism? Not necessarily. Indeed, a revived and renewed connectionalism can come through radical agency downsizing, considerable decentralization, and new patterns of mission, ministry, program, and witness.
>
> *Dr. Russell E. Richey, Duke Divinity School*

Let us say again that our organizational structure, our rules, do not create our connectionalism; they express our connection. We have limited our discussion to consideration of a changed structure rather than engaging in a theological discussion, simply because we affirm our Wesleyan theological heritage as the basis for our church. We believe that our proposal is absolutely congruent with our received Wesleyan theology. Our structure needs to be more congruent with our theology, but a changed structure in no way means a destroyed connection.

I do not really fear a future in which a renewed Methodism deliberately ventures the loss of its denominational existence. My fears have to do with two other, greater, dangers. The first is a Methodism that tries to hold itself as intact as possible (as we have been inclined to do for the past half-century)—in which case we will slowly but surely lose ourselves in a bad cause. The second is a Methodism that has forgotten that polity is never more than a mere instrument to the real mission of every church, Methodist or any other: that the world may hear the gospel, may come to believe that Jesus Christ is our common Lord and Savior, may truly come to newness of life in the Holy Spirit and so be saved!

Dr. Albert Outler, 1968 (in a speech reported by Angus M. Brabham III in The South Carolina Methodist Advocate, *18 January 1968, 8-9)*

Our proposals for a decentralized connection raise great fear among many. Several pastors claim that the result of such proposals cannot be called a connection. We disagree. We are connected by the common call we have heard from

Jesus Christ, "Come, follow me." We are connected by our love for one another as we serve in Christ's name. We are held together by the fellowship of mission, by the leadership of our bishops, by the unity of worship, and by our disciplined life together. We are united by

1. our name: The United Methodist Church
   — recognized and loved by many

2. our heritage as part of the Wesleyan revival
   — a unique blend of social and personal piety

3. our symbol: the cross and flame
   — recognized worldwide as symbolizing a church linking warm, heartfelt piety and earnest social witness

4. appointment making by the bishops
   — our historic connection
   — pastors are a function of the mission of the church, not employees of local congregations

5. annual conferences
   — yearly celebrations of the ministry of clergy and congregations

6. credentialing of clergy
   — clergy responsibility for the training and credentialing of fellow clergy

7. connectional ownership of property
   — a visible and legal sign of our society

8. General Conference
   — a four-year binding together of our global connection

9. all the future efforts we will choose to continue
   — missions, global and national, evangelism, outreach, and other historic forms of Christian witness

10. General Board of Pension and Health Benefits
    — working together to care for our clergy and their
    families
11. our *United Methodist Hymnal* and *United Methodist Book
    of Worship*
    — we are a singing church, a church held together by
    word and sacrament in the praise of God
12. core structures
    — for example, trustees in each congregation; commit-
    tee on superintendency in each district; board of
    ordained ministry in each annual conference
13. United Methodist Women, Men, and Youth
    — organizations dedicated to service
14. our bishops
    — those who represent, in their person and in their
    leadership in worship and in meetings, the unity
    and apostolicity of the church

Many denominations have not only survived but pros-
pered with denominational structures much less centralized
than our own. Unfortunately, too often what we have
labeled as "connectionalism" has meant centralized, top-
down coercion, an organization sanctioned by one segment
of North American culture, and a form that has proved
unsuitable in a variety of cultural situations. Rules and
mandates issued from the top do not make a connectional
church. Our connection cannot be based upon distrust and
legalistic demands. It must be expressed as local churches
drawn together by common mission—common mission
owned and joyfully supported by each congregation. We
affirm ¶ 112.3 of our *Discipline* and its elucidation of the
theology of the "connectional principle" as the basis for the
renewed and reformed structure which we propose here.

Does our model take seriously corporate sin, especially
the sins of racism and sexism? In one sense, our present

structure assumes that our sin can be eradicated through law, rather than gospel: by the right application of rules, quotas, and funding rather than by persuasion, conversion, and right living. Until now we have let the general church fight these issues and ignored the reality of sin as manifested in our local congregations. We assuaged our guilt through quadrennial slogans. We created a permanent General Commission on the Status and Role of Women rather than appoint strong women to strong congregations. We attempted to pacify legitimate ethnic minority concerns with the creation of the General Commission on Religion and Race rather than through the struggle for racial justice in local congregations.

We must trust God to work within local United Methodist churches to create a visible, vibrant, and just witness to the inclusiveness of God's love. Too often, the attitude of our church has been, "We have these quotas, these mandated funds—isn't that enough?" Responsibility must be returned to the pastors and the local congregations for embodying the demands of the gospel within their life together. Our present system, rather than empowering women and ethnic minorities, disempowers these groups, as certainly as it disempowers all laity and clergy who are forced to rely upon the law rather than upon the gospel, and whose energies are dissipated in service of the system rather than participation in the mission of the church. We have demonstrated that we cannot as a church address the legitimate criticisms and aspirations of ethnic minorities in our present structure. A new, more adaptable, simplified, and localized structure is necessary.

Will competent but uncharismatic pastors suffer in a new system of clergy accountability? Possibly. We believe that competence will be recognized and affirmed in the congregation. Clearly, our present toleration of incompetent pastors will end. No congregation will want them, and no bishop will be able to justify their continued employment in a system that answers to the mission of the local church. Those pastors who have based their ministry upon service to the system, rather than to the edification and empowerment of the congregation, will have to refocus their ministry. Accountability to the mission of the local church—rather than flattering the managers of the system—must become the basis of our clergy evaluation and appointment. Some of our pastors, who may have been attracted to the present system of clergy deployment with its tendency to reward mediocrity, will be impressed with the need either to sharpen their skills or to find other employment. But we trust the local congregations to recognize and to affirm the faithful ministry of the majority of our clergy.

Minor tinkering with the system, modifying the national church structure only slightly, downsizing what we already have to save some money but not to focus our mission, will only increase our difficulties, not solve them. The proposals we have heard thus far from the General Council on Ministries seem to us like mere superficial rearrangement of the same system, perpetuating the same old problems. They do not constitute fundamental change. As one South Central Jurisdiction bishop has said, such proposals actually "add layers of bureaucracy" and sustain "the same component parts." Some voices at the 1996 General Conference will defend the status quo, cry racism or sexism or congregationalism in the hope of silencing debate on renewal, and attempt to drive out the reformers with charges of disloyalty. How can these voices receive a credible hearing, when statistics show that our present system has driven out so many ethnic persons, women, men, young adults, and youth and weakened the power and witness of our connection? At a time when our quotas and top-down mandates were supposed to be creating a more just and inclusive church, we lost at least a million women as members. Ethnic growth was disappointing, particularly among our African American constituency. We tried to solve at the top the problems that should have been solved through evangelism and inclusiveness at the local church level. The current system should be judged on the basis of its fruits rather than on the basis of abstract assertions and pious platitudes.

Connectionalism does not mean subservience to a hierarchical bureaucratic leadership. It does not mean a vast bureaucracy which is unquestioningly funded by the local churches. It does not mean lay toleration of unproductive and incompetent clergy simply because the bishop and cabinet refuse to make tough decisions. It does not mean preservation of the institution as the first benevolent priority for our local churches. It does not mean some paternalistic system of coercion that is based upon distrust. *Connectionalism* means churches in the Wesleyan tradition working together, interdependent in mission, held together by their common commitment to preach and to embody the good news of Jesus Christ.

In our extensive meetings with pastors and laity, a number of folk have asked whether our political stance is right-wing Republican—some ecclesiastical form of the "Contract with America"—or free-for-all libertarian. Others ask if our theological stance is liberal (pluralistic) or conservative (back to Wesley). The questions reveal the difficulty most of us have in thinking through these matters without reducing them to "either/or" polarities. We have intentionally refused to limit ourselves to a certain political (we are both lifelong Democrats) or theological camp (we think of ourselves as strongly Wesleyan, sacramental activists). Neither of us has membership in Good News or the Methodist Federation for Social Action.

We know, from our many conversations with others, that

our proposals transcend the liberal and conservative labels. We know that women and men, persons of all colors and regions will hear in what we say a hopeful word that speaks to their dissatisfaction with our present system. Our goal is to liberate each congregation to serve Jesus Christ uniquely in its own setting.

The Wesleyan movement has no particular prejudice toward any institutional embodiment except toward that institutional arrangement which enables us to fulfill our theological mandate to "spread scriptural holiness throughout the land." We are practical people. Our connectionalism ought to be understood theologically rather than institutionally. Our present system is a historical creation, a relatively recent construction. We invented it for certain timely concerns, and we can change it in the interest of reinvigorated mission. The bonds which unite us are not those of church rule books but rather those of common commitment to the spreading of the good news of Jesus Christ.

Originally, our *Discipline* was lean on rules and regulations and thick with doctrine and belief. For years, Methodism lived outside of an established church, seeing itself not so much as a church but rather as a movement. A movement trusts people. An institution demands that the people trust the institution. In a movement, theological concerns provide the energy for the structure. In an institution, structure can too easily replace substance.

United Methodists participate in the heritage of the Wesleyan revival of religion in eighteenth-century England, a revival which eventually "spread scriptural holiness throughout the land," indeed over the whole world. We are bound by ties of mutual affection, by our beloved hymns and warm worship, by our commonsense approach to the alleviation of human suffering, by our practical theology which wants to put our beliefs into practice, by our faith that it is Jesus Christ, not our structure, who preserves the church. These factors unite us. A part of us has been reluctant to expend so many pages criticizing our present institutional structure. We do not want to encourage an already overmanaged, overorganized church to expend any more energy than is absolutely necessary in considering rules, regulations, and structure. Nonetheless, we believe we have put forward a helpful alternative to our present system. We are convinced that the present rules and regulations must be changed, and changed now, if we are to keep up with the movements of a living Lord, if we are to continue to have our part in the expanding reign of God. By God's grace and the loving intrusions of the Holy Spirit, we shall. The new creation that shall arise from the restrictive structural cocoon in which we now exist shall be more wonderful than anything we can now imagine.

Notes

Introduction

1. William H. Willimon and Robert L. Wilson, *Rekindling the Flame: Strategies for a Vital United Methodism* (Nashville: Abingdon, 1987), 9. Among the strategies for renewal proposed in that book were the following: recover the real purpose of the church, affirm the Wesleyan heritage, serve the church instead of the clergy, demand leaders instead of managers, abolish the minimum salary for clergy, insist that the clergy teach in the parish, simplify the local church structure, trust the laity, and give priority to Sunday morning. Our impression was that *Rekindling the Flame* was better received by laity than clergy, with the exception of younger clergy. Clergy, particularly those who have benefited from the status quo, have more to risk in changing the present structures. Our impression was that *Rekindling the Flame* was not implemented because the national denomination, particularly its leaders, was still in denial that the crisis was really a crisis. We believe that denial is no longer possible and that there is a new willingness to move forward.

2. Dr. Outler's speech was reported by Angus M. Brabham III in *The South Carolina Methodist Advocate*, 18 January 1968, 8-9.

1. Revitalize the Connection

1. The prediction in William H. Willimon and Robert L. Wilson, *Rekindling the Flame* (Nashville: Abingdon, 1987) proved to be all too accurate:

Revitalization tends not to come from those who hold positions of authority and power in an institution. . . . persons in the institutional hierarchy and bureaucracy will find genuine reform too threatening to their present positions. . . . Change requires redistribution of power, and those who have power want to preserve it. (22-23)

2. *Rekindling the Flame,* 23.

2. Empower the Local Church

1. William H. Willimon and Robert L. Wilson, *Rekindling the Flame: Strategies for a Vital United Methodism* (Nashville: Abingdon, 1987), 51. The seniority system not only fails to serve our congregations, but it also demoralizes some of our best younger clergy.

Every time a bishop or district superintendent tells a pastor, "even though your gifts equip you to serve that church, I can't send you there yet because the salary is too high," or "You are going to that church because you are now making $15,000, and that church pays $15,500," they demoralize the most effective clergy and reinforce the notion of the least effective that it makes little difference what they do in a congregation—the system will keep them and promote them regardless of their work. The unwritten, unprescribed, and unlegislated clergy seniority system is demoralizing the church and its clergy. (52)

4. Reform the General Church

1. Quoted by the Reverend Ned Owens, Western North Carolina Conference.

2. This seemed to be a major finding of a 1993 study by our own Office of Research in the General Council on Ministries, as reported in "United Methodists Survey Themselves," *The Christian Century,* 25 August–1 September 1993, 813: "institutions in periods of decline come to take on certain characteristics. One such characteristic is to become increasingly focused internally instead of externally. Thinking and decision-making begin with maintenance questions."

3. Dennis Campbell, in Duke Divinity School Project on United Methodism and American Culture newsletter *Leadership Letters* 1, no. 1 (February 1995).

4. Ronald E. Vallet and Charles E. Zech, *The Mainline Church's Funding Crisis: Issues and Possibilities* (Grand Rapids, Mich.: Eerdmans, 1995), 48-49.

5. Ibid., 100-108.

Index

139